OUR ANCESTORS WERE BRICKMAKERS AN

A history of the Corder and related families in the clayworl

———

by

Adrian Corder-Birch

with photographs, photo restoration and illustrations by Christine Walker

The Brick, Tile and Pottery Works at Southey Green, Sible Hedingham circa 1914
when owned by Harry Corder

© Adrian Corder-Birch 2010

Published by Adrian Corder-Birch
Rustlings
Howe Drive
Halstead
Essex
CO9 2QL

Email: corder-birch@lineone.net

All rights reserved. No part of this publication may be reproduced or transmitted in any form or by any means, electronic or mechanical, including photocopying, recording, or any information storage and retrieval system, without permission in writing from the publisher.

Printed by The Lavenham Press Limited
Arbons House
47 Water Street
Lavenham
Suffolk
CO10 9RN

ISBN 978-0-9567219-0-7

Further copies of this book are available from the Author/Publisher as above

Price £14.95 plus postage and packing

Cheques and postal orders in English pounds sterling, payable to Adrian Corder-Birch

CONTENTS

Page

Authors preface	5
Acknowledgements	7
Foreword	9
A brief introduction to the craft of brickmaking by hand	11
Corder family tree	12

Chapters

1	John Corder (1806-1880) and his early years in Gestingthorpe	13
2	John Corder at Castle and Sible Hedingham	17
3	William Corder (1835-1903) and Southey Green Brick, Tile and Pottery Works, Sible Hedingham	23
4	Harry Corder (1873-1942) and Southey Green Brick, Tile and Pottery Works	35
5	John Corder (1876-1922)	53
6	Fred Corder (1885-1961)	57
7	Potter's Hall Brick Works, Great Yeldham	63
8	Park Hall Road Brick Works, Gosfield	67
9	George Corder (1863-1938) and his sons William Dan Corder (1886-1970) Herbert Charles Corder (1888-1970) and Walter Edward Corder (1896-1983)	71
10	Brick Kiln Hill Brick Works, Castle Hedingham, Robert Corder (1833-1915) and family	83
11	John Corder (1863-1957) and his three sons Edward John Corder (1886-1938), Bert William Corder (1889-1955) and Percy James Corder (1896-1989)	93
12	Edward Corder (1868-1940) and the Manor Brick Works, Thundersley	105

13	David Corder (1837-1881), James Corder (1840-1907) and Alfred Corder (1845-1898)	111
14	Henry Corder (1850-1934)	115
15	Related brickmaking family from Castle Hedingham: Samuel Westrop (1830-1867) and Alfred Westrop (1853-1879)	117
16	Related brickmaking families from Sible Hedingham:	
	Boreham family	119
	Brett, King and Gepp families	120
	Willett family	122
	William James Wiseman (1882-1959)	124
17	Related brickmaking families from Gestingthorpe:	
	Finch family	125
	Felton family	129
	Rippingale family and Harry Rippingale (1889-1978)	131
18	Finch Brick Works at Hull, Yorkshire	135
19	Friendly Societies including Oddfellows	139
20	Raymond John Corder and Adrian Corder-Birch	143

Glossary	147
Bibliography, sources, notes and references	150
Index	163

AUTHOR'S PREFACE

This is a history of those members of the Corder and related families who were associated with the brick, tile, pipe and pottery making industry, mainly in central north Essex, during the last two hundred years. It also includes a few members of those families who were associated with allied trades such as bricklayers, builders and even two carpenters who made brick and tile moulds. This is principally a family history rather than a detailed account of brickmaking, however where relevant some information about brickmaking and its history is included.

The information and illustrations in this book have been collected during a period of well over forty years. My research commenced in 1967 when I was a pupil at Hedingham School and our Geography Teacher, Cleone Branwhite, asked our class to prepare a project upon some aspect of the local economy or industries as part of our CSE geography examination. Many in the class chose various local farms to study for a year but I wanted to find a different subject. It was my mother, Beatrice Birch, to whom this book is dedicated, who suggested that I research the local brickmaking industry.

I had been aware from a young age that her father, grandfather and uncles had been brickmakers. I knew the whereabouts of some of the former Hedingham brickworks where I had been taken by my mother during footpath walks around the Hedinghams during my early years. Without hesitation I agreed to my mother's suggestion to study these brickworks and I cycled and walked many miles around the Hedinghams and surrounding villages taking photographs of the sites of these brickworks. Some of these photographs, taken over forty years ago, appear in this book and show the remains of kilns, drying sheds and other buildings, many of which have since been demolished - and old clay pits, which were later filled in. In particular I visited Bulmer Brick and Tile Works, where bricks were, and still are, made by hand in the traditional way and where one member of the Corder family was still working until 2008.

I interviewed many people including relatives and former brickmakers and recorded their memories. This initial research resulted in my first publication about the history of the brickmaking industry in the Hedingham area for which I was paid the sum of five guineas, which was a generous sum for a 15 year-old student in 1968. (1) Having passed my CSE with grade 1, I continued to collect information and further publications followed. (2) In 1978 I became a member of the British Brick Society and of the British Archaeological Association and in particular its Brick Section. Since 1989 I have been Hon. Auditor of the British Brick Society and am now one of its longest serving officers.

Many years ago the late Ned (Edgar) and Arkie (Alfred) Spurgeon of Sible Hedingham introduced me to a village builder, Bill (William) Martin, who now lives at Cresswells Farm. He told me that the name of Corder was synonymous with brickmaking in the Hedinghams. During my research I found that my Great Grandfather, William Corder, owned three brickworks and other members of the family managed two more brickworks and were employed in several others. Edward Corder was even granted a patent for a new roofing tile. Over forty years later and with many diversions in the meantime, this book is well overdue and is a record of the Corder and related families and their association with the clay working industry.

My great, great grandfather, John Corder and his direct descendants worked a total of about six hundred years in the industry during a period of just over one hundred years. The craft and skill of brickmakers and potters was often passed down from father to son; there are many examples of three and four generations following the trade and marriages between brickmaking families. The work was hard and heavy, the hours long, especially for those engaged in piece work who regularly made over a thousand bricks a day by hand. Although the pay was usually better than for agricultural workers, until the introduction of pensions many brickmakers worked until their deaths. Some master brickmakers, including William Corder, had other business interests such as farming to supplement their incomes.

Some buildings survive incorporating clay products as a permanent memorial to their craftsmanship. Unfortunately, little remains of many of the brickworks featured in this book. Although it mainly records brickworks owned and managed by the Corder family and refers to members of the family employed in other brickworks it is not a complete history of all the brickworks in the area. Abbreviated family trees have been included to show various relationships but these have mainly been restricted to those associated with the clayworking industry and therefore do not show all family members. Many of the maps used have been reduced in scale and with the exception of the map of Warren's Farm, the usual convention of north being at the top has been followed. The use of abbreviations has largely been avoided except for ERO for Essex Record Office. A glossary of terms used appears at the back of the book. Measurements are recorded in the imperial and not the metric system and similarly all amounts are pre-decimal. There is a detailed bibliography, sources, notes and references section at the end of the book, which corresponds with the numbered sequence in each chapter where the reference numbers are enclosed in brackets.

Although the majority of the book details John Corder and his descendants, the later chapters cover more distant relations involved in the industry.

If anyone can add any information or have any more photographs or documents I should be pleased to hear from you.

Adrian Corder-Birch

Rustlings
Howe Drive
Halstead
Essex CO9 2QL

18th June 2010

ACKNOWLEDGEMENTS

The principal sources of information, loan of photographs and help came from numerous relations. It is very sad to recall that several have passed away since I commenced this work, namely:

Beatrice and Wilfred Birch (my late parents), Alfred and Gladys Corder (of Halstead), Charles and Maud Corder (of Bocking), Edward D. Corder (whom I visited in Canada in 1981), Edith E. M. (May) Corder (of Sible Hedingham), Edith M. Corder (of Earls Colne), Percy and Edith E. Corder (of Sible Hedingham), Sarah Corder (my grandmother), Walter and Ethel Corder (of Castle Hedingham), William D. Corder (of Sible Hedingham), Margery Foster (nee Corder), Sybil Halls (nee Corder), William Heels (son of Mary Corder), Harry and Lily Rippingale (nee Corder), Fred Rippingale (son of Ellen Corder of Gestingthorpe), Len Smith (son of Ellen Corder of Castle Hedingham), William Willett (youngest brother of Alice Ann Corder), Winifred Goodwin (nee Bristow) daughter of George and Edith Bristow (nee Downs) and Bertram Hogarth (my father in law).

I was also assisted by the following, who are not related, but have also died since my research commenced:

Harry (Higgler) Broyd, John (Jack) Cornell, Albert and Gladys Finch (of Gestingthorpe), Sir Ronald Long, Kt., Jack Lindsay (the author), Lawrence Minter (former owner of Bulmer Brick Works), Cecil and Dorethea Pannell (of Gestingthorpe), George H. Rayner (last owner of Maiden Ley Brick Works, Castle Hedingham) and Mary Rayner (his sister), Phyllis Rayner (formerly of Gestingthorpe and latterly of Gosfield), William Raynham, Albert Redgewell (burner at The Sible Hedingham Red Brick Company Limited), Norman Ripper, Stephen Ripper, Winifred Ripper, James Ruggles (for information about Potters Hall Brick Works, Great Yeldham), Alfred J. (Arkie) Spurgeon, Edgar J. (Ned) Spurgeon and Stanley Springett.

Fortunately some contributors from whom I have received information and photographs are still with us and I am particularly grateful to the following:

Charles Bird, Ashley Cooper, Harold Cooper, Doug Corder (Canada), Capt. Edward (Jim) Corder, R.C.N., (Canada), Kenneth Corder, Victor Gray, M.A., (former County Archivist), Arthur Laver, Gladys Lewis, Peter Minter (of Bulmer Brick Works), Doreen Potts, Richard Shackle (former Librarian) Hubert Springett and Gayle Thomson (nee Corder of Canada).

Four of my former teachers were also particularly helpful namely Cleone Branwhite, Frederick W. Pawsey, D.F.C., J.P., Dorothy Smith and the late Harry Theedom, M.B.E. It was Dorothy Smith who passed on recollections of conversations with Alice Drury (nee Corder).

The photographs used were copied by John Abbott, Kenneth Stanhope, Christine Walker, the late Harry Cole and the late Arthur Morgan, to all of whom I would like to express my appreciation.

I have carried out a vast amount of research in the Essex Record Office whose archivists and staff were always most helpful as were the staff in Colchester Central Library and other libraries in Essex and London. The maps were copied from originals at the Essex Record Office, Colchester Central Library and the Map Room at the British Museum, later transferred to the British Library. Members of the Archaeology Section (as it then was) of Essex County Council have assisted, notably Shane Gould.

I would particularly like to record my appreciation to Dave Osborne, Geoffrey Root and Liz Tolfts and other former staff at the 'Halstead Gazette' for allowing me to peruse back copies of this very informative newspaper. These are now in the care of Doreen Potts who has kindly continued to allow access to this valuable resource.

I also wish to record my thanks to members of the British Brick Society and the Brick Section of the British Archaeological Association for information and support, particularly to Patrick Crouch, Michael Hammett, Dip. Arch., A.R.I.B.A., David Kennett, Ann Los, Graeme Perry, Terry Smith, the late C. H. (Bill) Blower and the late Angela Simco (Consultant Archaeologist).

The following have graciously given permission to reproduce illustrations, namely Malcolm Root, G.R.A., for his painting on the front cover, the Essex Record Office for various maps and documents, the British Museum, the British Library and Colchester Central Library for the remaining maps. I am also grateful to the British Library Newspaper Library for permission to reproduce illustrations from the British Clayworker and the Brickbuilder. Two local authors also gave permission for short quotes from their books namely the late Jack Lindsay from 'The Discovery of Britain' and Ashley Cooper from no less than three of his books.

I should like to record my grateful thanks to my wife, Pam, for her support, encouragement and help, and to my sister, Christine Walker, for her expertise with photography, photo restoration and copying illustrations to enhance this book. Pam, Christine and her husband Phil have also read the proofs and suggested helpful improvements, which has been much appreciated. Pam has also endured many hours on her own whilst I have been 'missing' researching and compiling this book. I have monopolised our computer, which is now available, once again, for Pam's use.

Finally, I should like to thank Peter Minter for writing the splendid Foreword and for checking and correcting the technical detail using his immense knowledge as a Master Brickmaker.

ADRIAN CORDER-BIRCH

2010.

FOREWORD

I am delighted to be able to contribute to this publication by way of the Foreword. Although it is essentially a family history it is also a history of the brickmaker's craft over some two hundred years. Initially it was a small but important part of the local economy, providing a fine product to the community close to where the brickworks was situated. However, the nineteenth century saw a mushrooming of the building industry, both in the rural areas, and the expansion of London. The Hedinghams were ideally placed to supply this growing market. There was an abundance of good clays, which were readily accessible, and a workforce who could be drawn from families long versed in the art of the brickmaker.

The Corder family was one such family, their skills being handed down over the generations. They could provide 'in house' all the requirements from mould making to kiln firing; from the clay preparation to brickmaking. The growth of the industry led to the extension of the railway which fuelled the demand, brickworks springing up throughout Essex. Two World Wars began the decline, so many of the skilled men failing to return, machines replacing man, a way of life disappearing. Now all this is lost and for the most part the people are forgotten, remembered only by the occasional road or field name. The brickworks sites can still be found, but many are now under housing and industrial estates.

Being in a tight knit brickmaking community meant that there would be many family connections, my own; new to the area when judged by the Corder family, certainly began its association with the sale of the Southey Green Brick Tile and Pottery Works in 1942. I attended the sale with my father, who seemed to buy unending lots. All of which required transporting back to Bulmer. Apart from a host of equipment, he purchased large numbers of 'green' bricks and tiles to be fired at Bulmer. These were loaded onto an old Leyland lorry. The weather was fine and hot, and it was slow work; on our way home we passed The Windmill at the top of the hill before going down into Sible Hedingham. Here was a small 'off licence' and a stop before returning to Bulmer was essential. Aged just under 9 years old I was deemed too young to partake of beer. However, I did qualify to have Ginger beer.

In the 1980's I employed young Raymond Corder, a direct Corder descendent. Brickmaking was 'in the blood' and he soon became first class at his trade, able to make numbers his forefathers would have been proud of. Numbering among them Harry Rippingale.

Adrian has further strengthened the tie with the passing to us of the main Southey Green pug mill, no longer in use, but preserved as part of brickmaking history.

Today, only two brickworks remain in Essex. Four in total in East Anglia! Together with the loss of small farms, so much of the bedrock of the rural society has vanished; Adrian's detailed research recorded here is invaluable to all who seek to understand their past and to all of us who need to maintain a future.

Peter Minter

Master Brickmaker, Member of the British Brick Society and the Institute of Clayworkers.
Director of The Bulmer Brick and Tile Co. Limited and of The Cambridgeshire Tile and Brick Company Limited
Hole Farm
Bulmer
Near Sudbury
Suffolk CO10 7EF

23rd April 2010

A brick made by John Corder (1806-1880) inscribed, *"J Corder October 27"*
He is the Great, Great Grandfather of Adrian Corder-Birch and Christine Walker and the progenitor of the majority of brickmakers detailed in this book.

A BRIEF INTRODUCTION TO THE CRAFT OF BRICKMAKING BY HAND

Traditionally, bricks could only be made, dried and fired during the spring, summer and autumn when there was no risk of frost, which would crack and break up a 'green' brick. During the winter months many men were laid off with no work, although a few were fortunate enough to find employment digging out clay by hand ready for the brickmaking season. They used an implement called a graft and were expected to dig out one cubic yard an hour.

The clay was left in a heap to weather and when required the good clay, which was free from stones, was put through a pug-mill. Any clay which contained stones was either discarded or washed in a wash-mill and later added to the other clay in the pug-mill. Water was added to make the clay the correct consistency and the 'pug' was placed on the brickmaker's table using a 'cuckle'. On the table was a 'stock' board on top of which was a 'filler', which formed the 'frog' in the brick. The stock board kept the mould, a mere frame without top or bottom, in position. The mould was sanded or wetted, to prevent the pug adhering to the sides and a warp of pug was then thrown into the mould with some force to fill the corners. The surplus was removed by pulling a 'strike', a piece of wood, or a bow with wire, across the top of the mould. The 'green' brick was placed on a pallet board and onto a cradle or 'off bearing barrow', which held about 30 bricks. When the barrow was full it was wheeled to the 'hacks', where the 'green' bricks were unloaded to dry. After a few days the bricks were 'skintled', that is turned round, in herringbone fashion so that the sun and wind could dry all surfaces.

When dry the bricks were loaded onto a kiln or crowding barrow and stacked in the kiln for burning. The majority of brickworks referred to in this book had kilns, although there is evidence of the clamp method of firing at a few locations in the area during earlier times. 'Up-draught' kilns were the most common although some brickworks used 'down-draught' kilns latterly. Kilns were originally wood fired until transportation improved and coal became available. Wood firing a kiln containing up to 20,000 bricks took about a week compared with three or four days using coal. (1) After cooling, the kiln was unloaded using the kiln or crowding barrow and the products were ready for sale.

(For more information about brick making terms, please see Glossary on page 149).

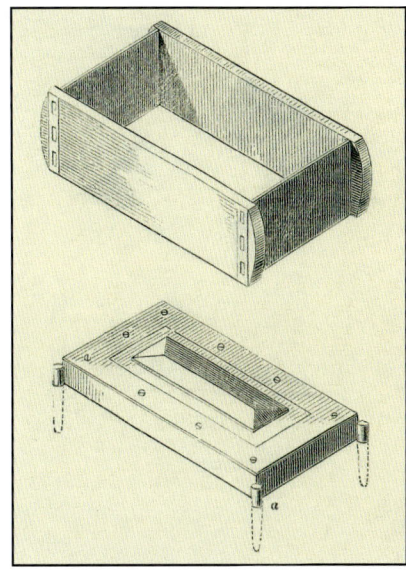

A brick mould and stock board

Descendants of William Corder

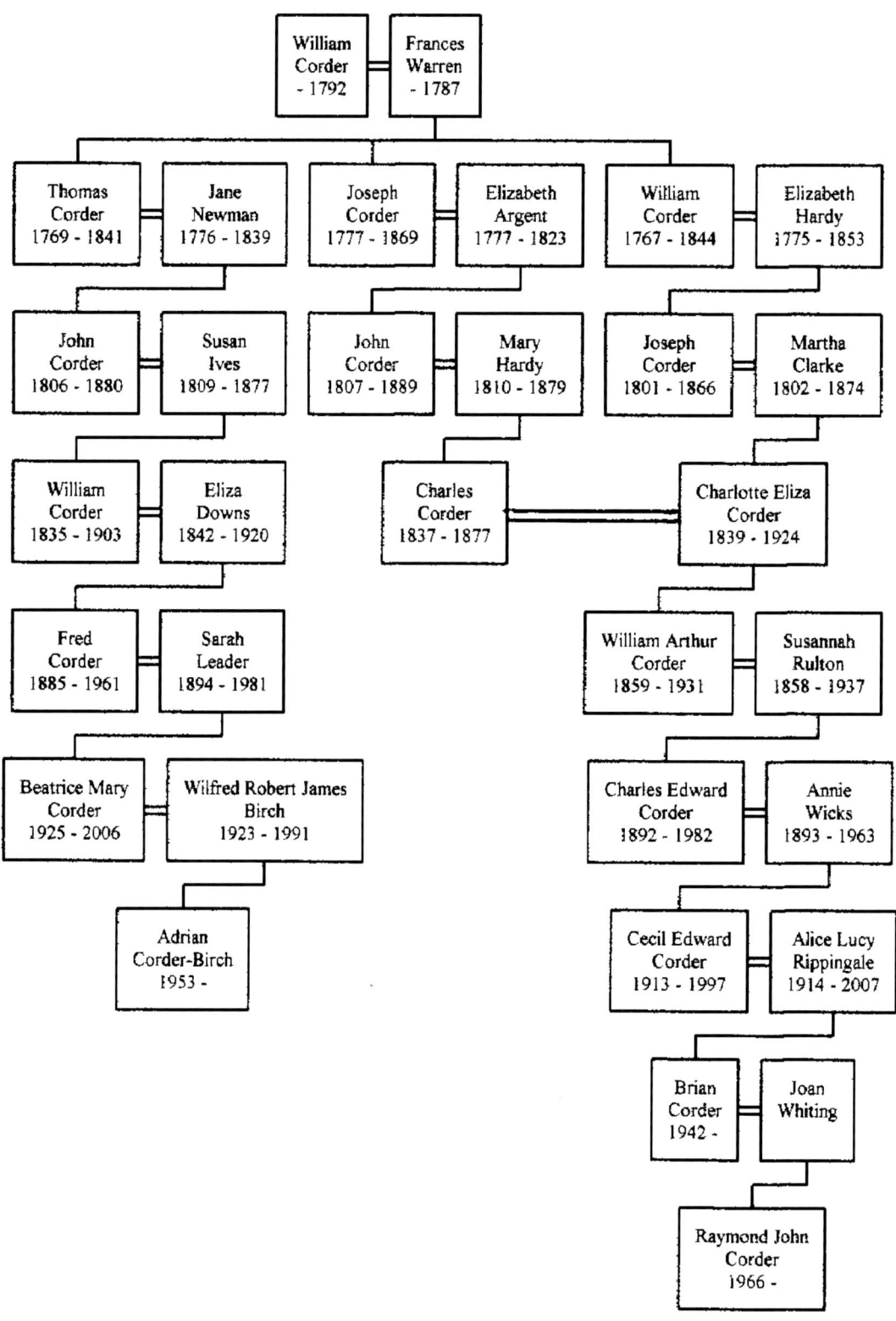

Chapter 1

JOHN CORDER (1806-1880) AND HIS EARLY YEARS IN GESTINGTHORPE

One of the first references to the Corder family in Gestingthorpe is the marriage of William Corder to Frances Warren in Gestingthorpe Church on 12th June 1766. They had ten children between 1767 and 1787. The youngest was a son, John, who was baptised in Gestingthorpe Church on 26th July 1787 on the same day as his mother, Frances Corder was buried at the west end of the Churchyard. William Corder was also buried there on 10th November 1792. (1)

It is through their second son, Thomas Corder (1769-1841) that the majority of brickmakers are descended. Thomas Corder married Jane Newman (c1776-1839) at Gestingthorpe Church in December 1800. (2) They had seven children, of whom their second son John Corder became the first known member of the family to be a brickmaker and potter.

John Corder was born at Gestingthorpe on 10th August 1806 and baptised in Gestingthorpe Church on 16th November 1806. (3) He married Susan Ives (1809-1877) a native of Little Yeldham, at Belchamp Walter Church on 5th February 1829. (4) They lived at Church Street Gestingthorpe where their first eight children were born. The first reference to John being a brickmaker is in the Gestingthorpe Baptism Register when their second son, William Corder, was baptised on 8th April 1835 which states that his father's occupation is *'Brickmaker'*. (5) John was later recorded as a *'Brickmaker'* living at Church Street, Gestingthorpe in the 1841 census. (6)

Throughout the majority of the nineteenth century there were two brickworks and a pottery in Gestingthorpe but it is not known at which of these John was employed. Bricks, tiles and pottery were manufactured continuously in Gestingthorpe from the beginning of the sixteenth century to 1951. The massive red brick tower of the Church was built during the 1520s with bricks made in the village and a Court Roll of 1562 refers to a Brick Kill (Kiln) Field. (7) The Rayner family were making bricks in the village by 1750 and continued until 1951. The Rayner, Downs and Finch families who owned brickworks and potteries in the village were very much inter-related and their ownership of these manufactories is rather complex. John Corder was probably employed by either John Rayner (1769-1843) and his successor or by John Downs (1769-1877). (8) (He was most likely employed by the latter because from about 1848 he was manager of a brickworks in Castle Hedingham for John Down's daughter in law - see chapter 2)

One Gestingthorpe brickworks, known as *'The Lower Yard'* and situated at Pot Kiln Chase, was in production by 1750 until about 1938. The other brickworks was known as *'The Upper Yard'* and as *'The Clamp'* and was north east of Delvyns Farm. Field names of *'The Clamp Piece'*, *'Clamp Glebe'* and *'The Clamp Earth Pits'* were recorded on a map of Gestingthorpe surveyed in 1804 (9) and repeated on the Tithe Map of 1838. (10) These names indicate early brickmaking sites with bricks being fired in a 'clamp' as opposed to a kiln, and manufacture continued (possibly intermittently) until final closure in 1951.

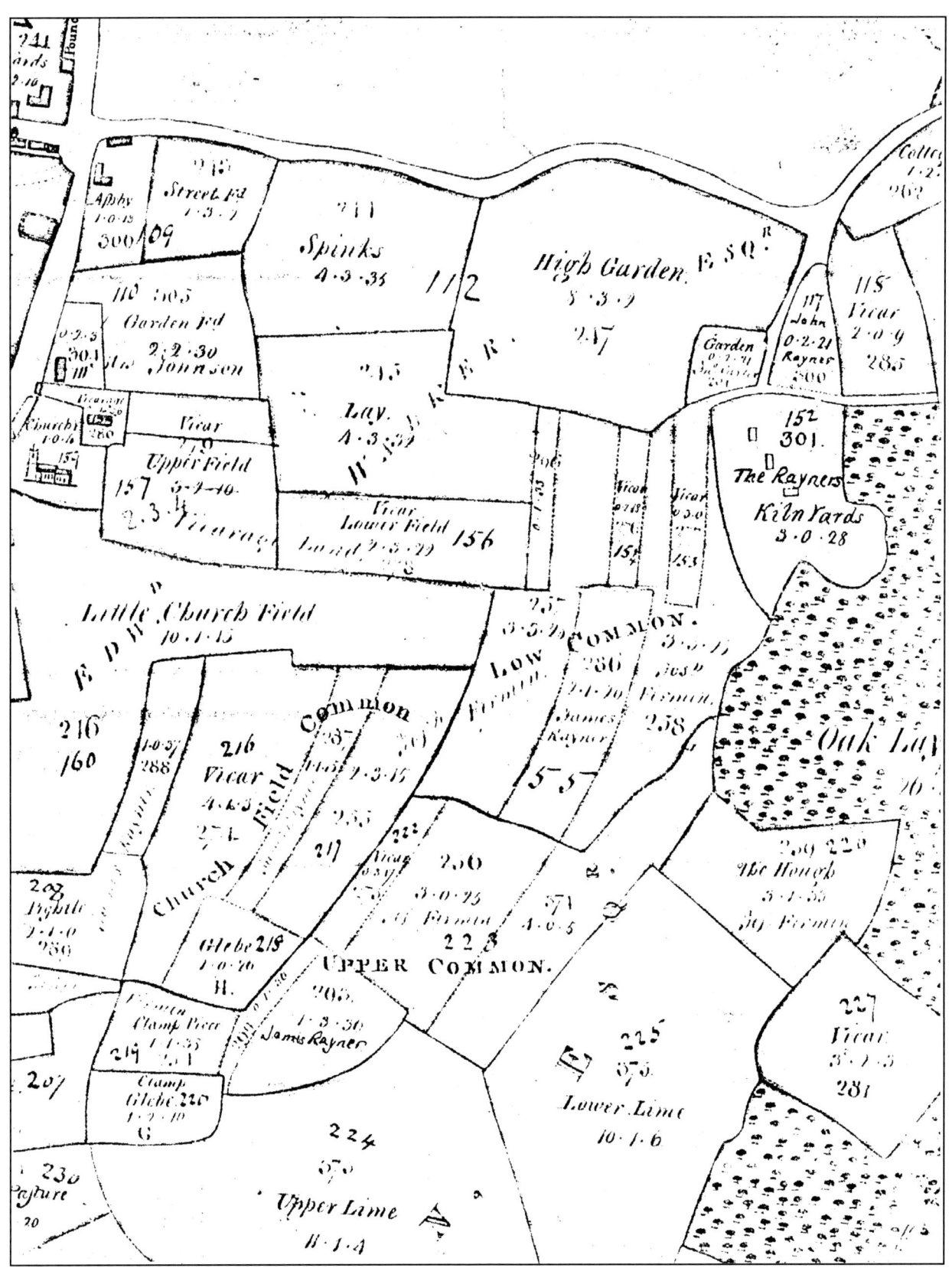

A map of Gestingthorpe surveyed in 1804 showing part of the estate owned by Edward Walker of Over Hall, Gestingthorpe. Note the Brick Works occupied by the Rayner family are described as *'The Rayners Kiln Yards'* and in Upper Common two fields known as *'Clamp Piece'* and *'Clamp Glebe'*. (Reproduced by courtesy of Essex Record Office ref: D/P 85/3)

'The Pottery' was located in *'The Lower Yard'* and was in operation by the early seventeenth century until 1912. When George Finch closed *'The Pottery'* that year, his son, George Herbert Finch (1877-1943) erected a Pot Kiln at *'The Upper Yard'* where he made pottery until 1939. (11)

It is interesting to note that whilst John Corder was working in Gestingthorpe as a brickmaker, Edward Abel Bingham (1799-1872) was also working in Gestingthorpe as a potter for three years from 1834 to 1837 and they no doubt knew each other from this time. In 1837 Edward Bingham and family moved to Castle Hedingham where his son, also Edward Bingham (1829-1916) became a well known ornamental potter. (12) There were many connections between the Bingham and Corder families, which are referred to in this book.

In about 1848 John Corder and family also moved from Gestingthorpe to Castle Hedingham. His siblings and their families remained in Gestingthorpe including a younger brother Edward Corder (1818-1896). (It is some of Edward's descendants who are featured in chapter 17).

An early photograph of a Gestingthorpe Brick Works. The names of the men and boys are unknown but note how young the boys appear to be. The wheelbarrow loaded with pipes is a kiln or crowding barrow and pamments (floor bricks) are standing in the foreground.

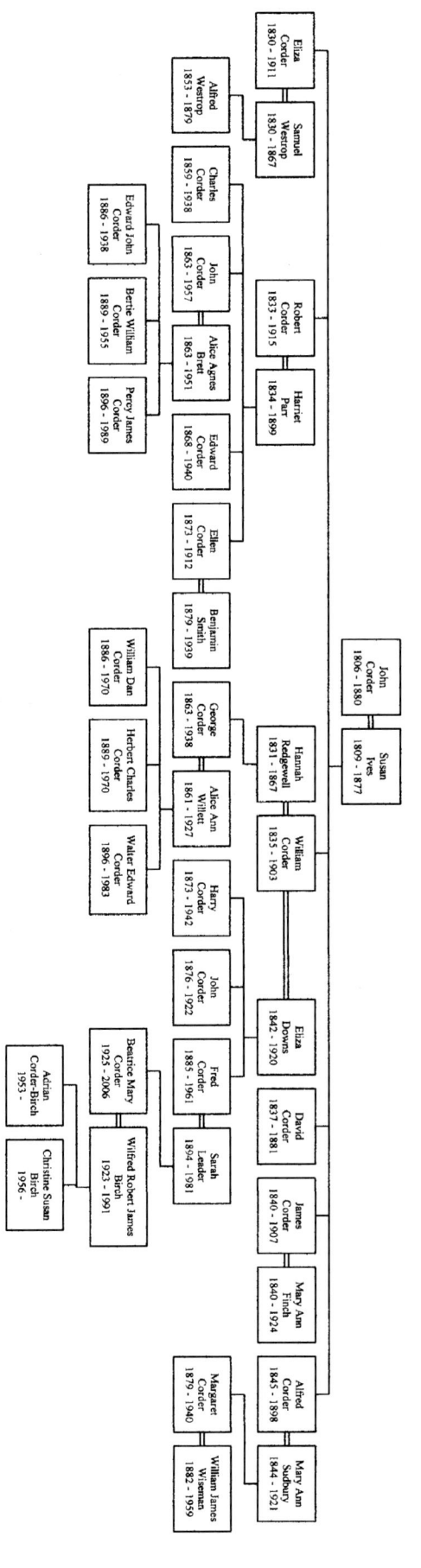

Descendants of John Corder

16

Chapter 2

JOHN CORDER AT CASTLE AND SIBLE HEDINGHAM

In about 1848 the Corder family moved into a cottage at Crouch Green, Castle Hedingham, one of a pair of cottages which overlooked the ancient Village Green, once the scene of many historic gatherings. In the mid nineteenth century these cottages were sometimes recorded under Nunnery Street such as in the 1851 census. (1) This census states that John was a *'brickmaker journeyman'* (2). It records that his four eldest sons, Robert aged 17, William 16, David 14 and James 11 were all *'brickmakers'*. It was common among many brickmaking families for sons to follow their fathers into the trade and this was the first of many such examples in the Corder family. John and his four sons were all employed at the brickworks at Brick Kiln Hill, Castle Hedingham, which was situated on the brow of the hill west of Crouch Green along the lane towards High Street Green, Sible Hedingham. This brickworks was then on the Hedingham Castle Estate and let to Sarah Ann Downs, who was proprietor from 1845 to 1855 and employed John Corder as her manager from about 1848.

The cottages at Crouch Green, Castle Hedingham, which were occupied by John Corder and family from circa 1848 and by his eldest son Robert Corder (1833-1915). They were later occupied by Robert's daughters namely Mary Dowsett (1865-1937), Ellen Smith (1873-1912) and their families. The cottages were sold by Frank Dowsett (1892-1974) (Mary's son) in 1944 and were therefore occupied by four generations of the Corder family and their descendants for nearly one hundred years.

Sarah Downs was the widow of William Downs (1821-1845) who was a son of John Downs (1796-1877), a master brickmaker of Gestingthorpe. (3) After making bricks in his father's brickworks in Gestingthorpe, William Downs moved to Castle Hedingham following his marriage to Sarah Ann Parker in 1842. He succeeded his father as proprietor of the brickworks at Brick Kiln Hill near Crouch Green in February 1845. Sadly William Downs died at Castle Hedingham later the same year at the young age of 24 years and his widow inherited and continued the business. Following the death of William, Sarah returned to live at Gestingthorpe where she is described in the 1851 census as a *'brickmaker'*. (4) From about 1848 John Corder managed this brickworks on her behalf.

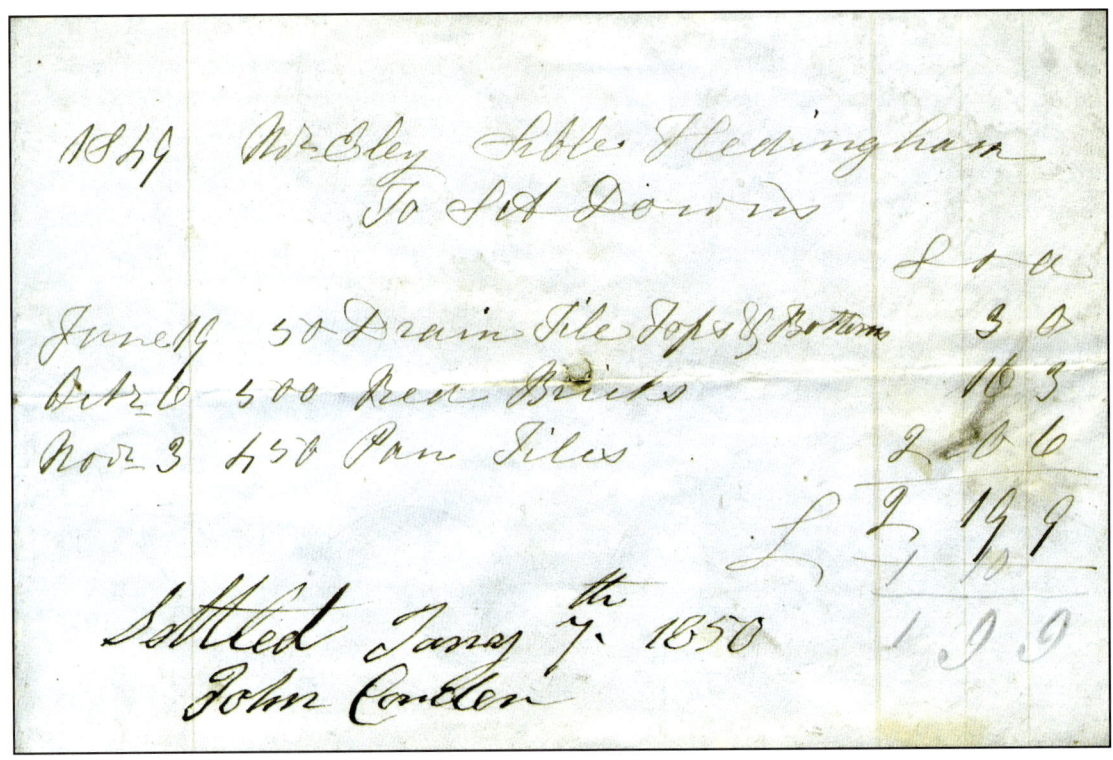

An invoice of 1849 for the supply of drain tiles, tops and bottoms, red bricks and pan tiles by S. A. Downs to Mr. Eley of Sible Hedingham

		£	s	d
June 19th	50 Drain Tile Tops & Bottoms		3	0
Oct 6th	500 Red Bricks		16	3
Nov 3rd	450 Pan Tiles	2	0	6
		2	19	9

This account was settled on 7th January 1850 and receipted by John Corder. (5)

In 1855 Sarah Ann Downs married John Hart of Gestingthorpe who assumed control of her brickworks, with John Corder continuing as manager for John Hart until about 1860. John Hart was originally farm bailiff to his sister, Mrs. Phoebe Downs and farmed Crouch House Farm, Gestingthorpe which then consisted of 92 acres. Their father William Hart was also a farmer in Gestingthorpe.

From 1784 duties (commonly known as the brick tax) were imposed on bricks and tiles (6). The initial rate was 2s 6d a thousand on all bricks and 3s 0d on most types of tiles but ridge and pan tiles were taxed at 8s 0d a thousand. These duties were increased in 1794 (7) to 4s 0d a thousand and 4s 10d on plain tiles but drain tiles became completely exempt. Another increase took place in 1803 (8) to 5s 0d a thousand on bricks only. Brickmakers were required to pay duty on the number of green bricks and tiles produced. In 1833 the duty on tiles was removed (9) and in 1850 the brick duty was completely repealed. (10). As manager it was necessary for John Corder to maintain a record of all green bricks made until 1850 so that the appropriate duty could be paid to the Commissioners of Inland Revenue. The above invoice of 1849 was one of the last to be rendered before the removal of the brick duty the following year. The relief from this burden, followed by the arrival of the Colne Valley and Halstead Railway in 1861 led to an increase in the use of bricks, the expansion of existing and the creation of new brickworks.

Drain pipes and drain tiles were made for farmers and landowners for land drainage, which increased following the invention of machine-made tiles circa 1840. This made the work cheaper and more efficient. Following the Public Health Act 1848, brickmakers made an increasing number of drain pipes for public health authorities for sewage disposal systems, which continued throughout the late nineteenth and twentieth centuries.

John Corder was a drain tile maker as well as a brick maker and potter. As shown in these photographs drain tiles had flat bottoms and separate arch shaped or semi circular tops. The tops often included small holes through which water could drain. They were used for draining fields before circular pipes were made. The account receipted by John Corder in 1850 records drain tiles tops and bottoms. His grandson, Harry Corder (1873-1942) later made circular drain pipes.

A pan tile inscribed *'April 12th 1851 John Corder Castle Hedingham Crouch Green'* was found on the roof of a barn at Nunnery Farm, Castle Hedingham during the mid twentieth century by builder, Percy James Corder (1896-1989), a great grandson of John, which is now in the possession of the author.

During the 1850s, Alfred Corder joined his father and four elder brothers and became a brickmaker. In 1853 their eldest sibling Eliza Corder (1830-1911) married Samuel Westrop (1830-1867) of Castle Hedingham who was also a brickmaker at Brick Kiln Hill Brick Works. Therefore during the mid 1850s John Corder, his five sons and a son in law were employed here, together with another John Corder (1832-1907) who was his first cousin once removed as shown in the following family tree.

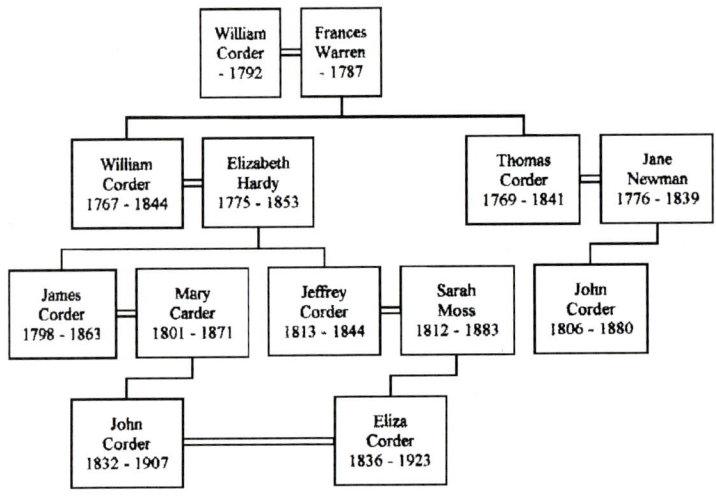

John Corder (1832-1907) who lived at Pye Corner, Castle Hedingham and later moved to London was son of James Corder (1798-1863) and Mary Corder formerly Carder (1801-1871). In 1854 John Corder married his first cousin, Eliza Corder (1836-1923) at the Baptist Church, Sible Hedingham when his occupation was recorded as a brickmaker. Eliza was the only child of Jeffrey Corder (1813-1844) and Sarah Corder formerly Moss (1812-1883). Following the death of Jeffrey, his widow married Charles Finch in 1846 and had two more children, Isaac and Elizabeth Finch. James and Jeffrey Corder were brothers and two of the sons of William Corder (1767-1844) and Elizabeth Corder formerly Hardy (1775-1853).

In about 1860 John Corder and family left Castle Hedingham and moved to Southey Green, Sible Hedingham, where his second son William had become a master brickmaker. In the 1861 census (11) John is recorded at Southey Green as a *'Brickmaker'* and in the same household are Alfred Corder and Henry Corder both *'Brickmaker's Labourers'*. In the 1871 census (12) John was still living at Southey Green but his occupation was recorded as *'Pot Maker'* (Potter) as was Henry Corder and a grandson, Alfred Westrop.

The early census returns reveal three members of the Corder family employed in the brickmaking industry as young as ten and eleven years of age. In 1851 James Corder was a *'Brickmaker'* by eleven years of age, in 1861 Henry Corder was a *'Brickmaker's Labourer'* at ten years of age and in 1871 Charles Corder was recorded as *'Helps Brickmaker'* aged eleven years. It is possible that they started full time work at younger ages but this practice ceased when 'The Factories and Workshop Act 1871' came into force. The Act provided that with effect from 1st January 1872:

"no child under the age of ten years, shall be employed in the manufacture of bricks and tiles, not being ornamental tiles, ..." (13).

This legislation is known to have applied to Edward Bingham's Pottery as well as to Brick and Tile Works in Sible and Castle Hedingham. It was necessary to regulate child and female labour in Brick, Tile and Pottery works throughout the country.

William Corder was sole proprietor of the Southey Green Brick, Tile and Pottery Works during the 1860s but during the 1870s John Corder went into partnership with his son when they traded as William and John Corder (14). John died at Southey Green Brickyard on 4th October 1880 and was buried on 9th October 1880 at Castle Hedingham Chapel Burial Ground aged 74 years. (15) It appeared that John Corder actively worked as a Potter until his death. An entry in a record book kept by Edward Bingham states:

"21st October 1880 Bought the late J. Corder's stock of Lead Clays & C."
(16).

John was a brickmaker and potter for at least forty five years. By 1942 John and his direct descendants (sons, grandsons and great grandsons only) had collectively worked for approximately six hundred years in the industry. This is a remarkable achievement for one family during a period of about one hundred years.

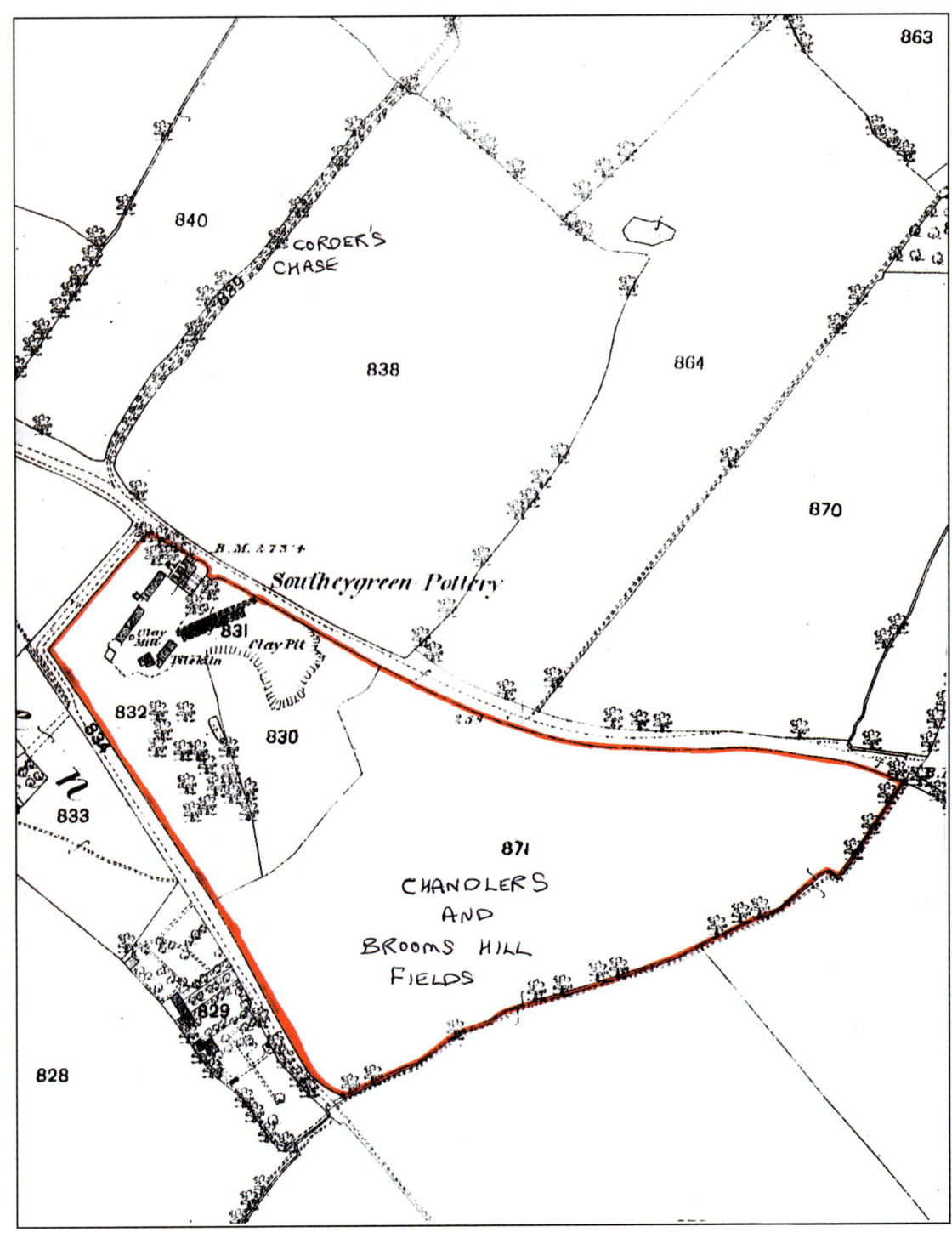

Southey Green Brick, Tile and Pottery Works (830, 831 & 832) when occupied by William and John Corder from the 1876 Ordnance Survey Map of 25 inches to 1 mile. The map shows the rows of hacks (above the number 831) correctly aligned north-east to south-west so that both sides of the hacks received an equal amount of sun and yet neither side was exposed to direct rays of sun around mid day. Corders Chase (839) from the Pottery to Sible Hedingham is shown between fields 838 and 840, which provided a more direct route to the village. Chandlers and Brooms Hill Fields (871) were farmed by William Corder.

Chapter 3

WILLIAM CORDER (1835-1903) AND SOUTHEY GREEN BRICK, TILE AND POTTERY WORKS AT SIBLE HEDINGHAM

William Corder was born at Gestingthorpe and baptised in Gestingthorpe Church on 8th April 1835, the second son of John Corder (1806-1880). William became a brickmaker at Gestingthorpe in the mid 1840's, being taught the trade by his father. This was before the family moved to Crouch Green, Castle Hedingham during or about 1848. In the 1851 census (1) William was recorded as a brickmaker aged 16 years living at Crouch Green. From about 1848 until 1859 he was employed as a brickmaker at Brick Kiln Hill Brick Works, Castle Hedingham, which was managed by his father.

William Corder (1835-1903)

In April 1859 William, then aged 24 years and still a brickmaker at Castle Hedingham, gave notice of marriage to Hannah Redgewell, who he married on 3rd June 1859 at Castle Hedingham Chapel. Following their marriage they moved to the long established Southey Green Brick, Tile and Pottery Works at Sible Hedingham, which William purchased from John Parish who had been its proprietor since 1835. William is recorded as occupier of a cottage, orchard, sheds and brick kiln at Southey Green and land near the brick kiln in the Land Tax Assessment from 1859-60 onwards. (2) The brickyard and adjoining farm land occupied by William Corder extended to 4a 2r 34p.

Earthenware production was in existence on this site by the early sixteenth century when *"the Cley Pitte"* was recorded in a rental of 1534, which gave its name to Clay Hall Farm, (3) adjacent to and immediately south west of the brickworks. This indicates clay extraction during the early sixteenth century but production could be much earlier. There is massive evidence of pottery making in this area of Sible Hedingham by the thirteenth century when the village was well known as a medieval pottery making centre. Since 1888 several kiln sites and large quantities of sherds have been found. These include kilns at Hole Farm (a short distance north east of Southey Green Brick, Tile and Pottery Works) first examined by Edward Bingham in 1888, which he probably combined with visits to the Corder family. Another kiln was discovered much later at Starlings Hill immediately east of the Corder works at Southey Green. The exact location was in the eastern corner of Chandlers Field, which had been previously occupied by William Corder for agricultural use. In March 1938 Norman Ripper discovered another potters kiln at Crows Cross, which was dated to the late thirteenth or early fourteenth centuries. In November 1972 Mrs. Lana Baines found an early medieval kiln and sherds of pottery in the garden of her home at Clare Cottage in the appropriately named Potter Street, recorded as '*Potterstrete*' by 1444. (4) There have also been finds at Hawkwood Manor, Potter Street and in nearby Lamb Lane in the vicinity of the former Tower Windmill. Kilns and pottery have also been discovered in Broaks Wood and around Foxborough Hill Farm. These kilns, which were mainly in production during the thirteenth century, made Hedingham Ware Jugs. (5).

In the centre of many of these former pottery kilns is Tile Kiln Farm, which name suggests medieval tile production. It was recorded as '*le Tyle Kyll*' in 1548 and as '*Tile-Kiln*' in 1768. (6) Tile Kiln Farm, between Broaks Wood and Crows Cross, is north east of the Corder Pottery at Southey Green. Amongst early documentary evidence of the Southey Green Brick, Tile and Pottery Works is a map of 1717 recording it as the Tile Kiln at South Green. (7) This was followed by numerous references to the Brick Kiln at Southey Green in manorial records throughout the eighteenth century when occupied by Thomas Walker and later Robert Harrington, both before 1784. They were followed by Thomas Osborne and Daniel Smith, who was admitted as tenant on the understanding that he would repair the kiln and erect a house on the site. In about 1802 John Hilton, a brickmaker, became proprietor of the brick kiln. His son, Charles Augustus Hilton, later owned the brickworks at Alderford Farm (8) As will be noted later, brick, tile and pottery making continued at Southey Green until the outbreak of the Second World War and the brickworks were sold in 1942. Therefore with a history of manufacturing here for well over four hundred years (albeit intermittently), it is one of the sites of longest duration in Essex.

In 1864 William Corder was one of the purchasers of items at the auction of the brickworks of the late Charles Augustus Hilton at Alderford Farm, Sible Hedingham. (9).

The account book for Thomas Eley, Maltster, Miller, corn, coal and hop Merchant of Tower Mill, Lamb Lane, Sible Hedingham records numerous purchases by William Corder. These include coal to fire the kiln, typical entries being:

'30th June 1868	Corder Wm.	7 ton 12 cwt. brights	£6 17s 9d
Paid Dec 12th	£6 17s 9d		
20th April 1869	Corder J & W	6 ton 12 cwt. brights	£5 19s 0d
Paid Jan 13th	£5 19s 0d		
20th July 1869	Corder Wm.	6 ton 3 cwt - best brights	£6 3s 6d
Paid January 13th	1870 £6 3s 6d'		

During the 1870s the account book also records the purchase of malt and hops by William Corder, to make beer for his employees, which was a component part of their earnings. William Corder also purchased hops and malt from George Bishop of Alderford Water Mill and typical entries from Bishop's account book are as follows:

'13th May 1889	W. Corder	1 sack malt	18s 0d
		4 th hops	4s 0d
22nd July 1889	W. Corder	1 sack malt	19s 0d
		4 th hops	4s 0d'

William Corder also made payments towards the Poor Rate in Sible Hedingham, which are recorded in the account book for the "Collection of Poor Rate for the Parish of Sible Hedingham". Typical entries being for the half year ending 29th September 1873 reveals that William paid two instalments of 11s 3d on 27th May and 5th July 1873.

Quite apart from the brickworks, William Corder also farmed land at Southey Green for many years until 1895. By the 1861 census (10) he was farming three and a half acres of land, which he was continuing to farm in 1871. In that year William was employing four men and three boys in the brickworks and pottery. (11). By 1869 William had taken his father, John Corder, into partnership and they traded as *William and John Corder, Brick Makers'* until the death of John in 1880. William then continued on his own account but employed his brother, Robert Corder (1833-1915) in the brickworks and pottery until sometime during the 1880s. (12) The land farmed by William was adjacent to his brickworks and pottery and the whole site extended to about four and three-quarter acres, with the brickworks, pottery and clay pits occupying about one and a quarter acres. Opposite the brickworks and pottery was *'Corder's Chase'* which was the Green Lane and public right of way from Southey Green across the fields to the village of Sible Hedingham.

In the Land Tax Assessments for the late 1870s until 1880, William and John Corder are recorded as occupiers of part of Southey Green Farm of which the proprietors were the Executors of John Savill. (13) The acreage or part of Southey Green Farm occupied by William and John Corder is not known.

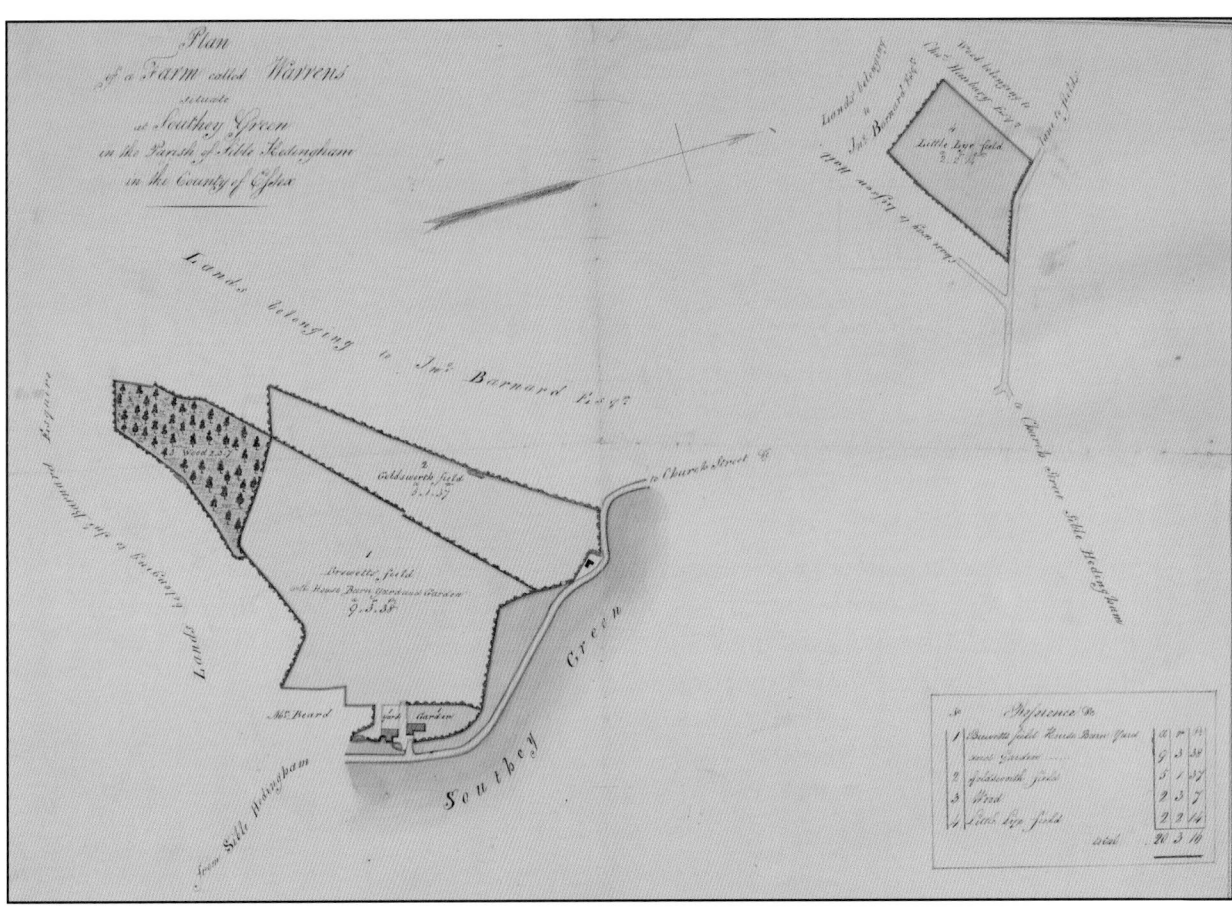

A nineteenth century map of Warrens Farm, Southey Green, which was occupied by William Corder until 1895. (Reproduced by courtesy of Essex Record Office ref: D/DBmT 109)

By the 1881 census (14) William was farming 25 acres of land and employing one man in agriculture. William took over Warren Farm at Southey Green sometime between 1871 and 1881, comprising just over twenty acres of which 2a 3r 7p was woodland and the remainder arable being three fields with a house, barnyard and garden. The largest field was Brewetts Field, which with the house, barnyard and garden extended to 9a 3r 38p. Immediately west of Brewetts Field was Goldsworth Field (also recorded as Goles or Goldings) of 5a 1r 37p. A little further away, just off the lane to Liston Hall Farm, was Little Lye Field (also known as Eleys Ley) of 2a 2r 14p. The latter was used for growing potatoes and the first two fields were *"good sound corn land"*. The small wood contained oak and other trees. The total acreage for Warrens Farm was 20a 3r 16p. The barn was *"timber built and thatched"* and there was also a *"horse shed"*. (15)

Warrens Farm of just over 20 acres together with his original holding of 3.5 acres and the brickworks and pottery of just over one acre amounted to a total acreage of 25 acres as verified by the 1881 census. (16) In addition William Corder had the right to use the sand pit on the Village Green at Southey Green at a rent of £1 0s 0d per annum. The right to use the sand pit was granted by successive owners of Hedingham Castle (as Lords of the Manor of Southey Green). In respect of the sand pit, William Corder was a yearly Michaelmas Tenant. (17)

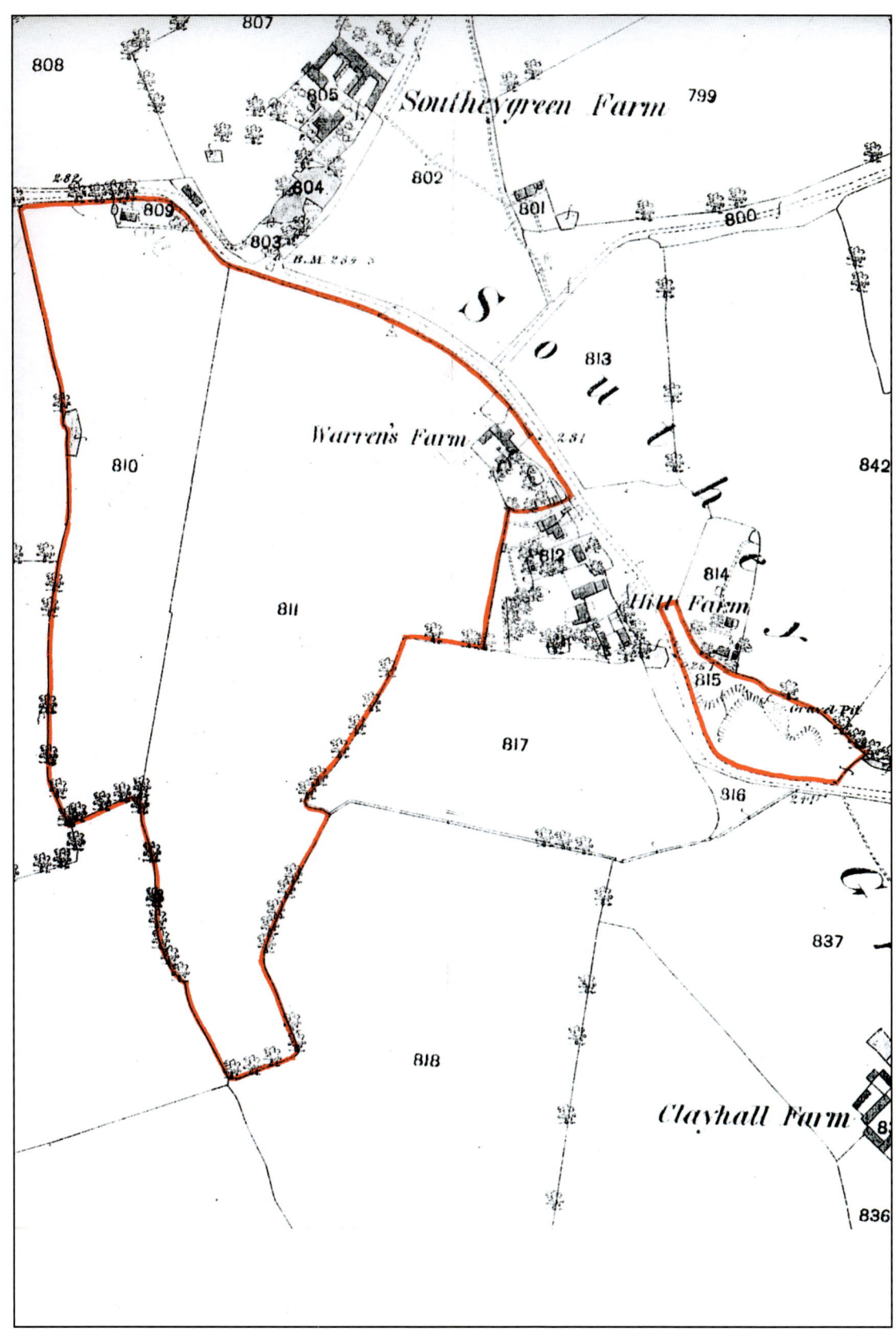

Warrens Farm (809, 810 & 811) and the Sand and Gravel Pit (815) at Southey Green; edged red, occupied by William Corder, from the 1876 Ordnance Survey Map, 25 inches to 1 mile.

The barn at Warrens Farm, Southey Green photographed by the author in 1985 prior to its conversion into a house.

The former sand pits at Southey Green

These sand pits were one of the last examples in Essex of a Master Brickmaker making an annual payment to a Lord of the Manor for the exclusive rights to excavate sand on a Village Green. William Corder and later his son Harry occupied these sand pits and used the sand at their brickworks. The remainder of the Village Green was Common Land for the benefit of all residents for recreation and grazing their animals. The site of the former sand pits can still be determined although much overgrown. Southey Green Village Green is now owned by Sible Hedingham Parish Council.

The view on the left indicates the depth of the pits and above the colour of the sand

In circa 1882, a further area of land at Southey Green was let to William Corder amounting to just over 10 acres. Therefore the total area of land occupied by him exceeded 35 acres including the brickworks, two houses and the farm buildings at Warrens Farm. In sale particulars of 1883 the 10 acres was described as *"Productive Arable Land"* called *"Chandlers and Brooms Hill"*, which was situated on the left side of the road leading *"from the Turnpike Road"* (the Sible Hedingham to Gosfield Road at Cut Maple) to Southey Green. The field numbers were 865, 866, 867, 868 and 868A. This land extended to 10a 2r 11p of which 3a 2r 32p was copyhold of the Manor of Prayors and the remainder was freehold. It was let to William Corder for £25 per annum. The owner of this property was John Cutts (18) who had acquired it on 29th September 1865. Following the death of John Cutts a dispute arose, which was heard in the Chancery Division of the High Court of Justice. The case of Re: John Cutts deceased's estate (Warren -v- Cutts) was commenced in 1882 and heard by Mr. Justice Kay in 1883 who ordered the sale of this and 22 other lots in Sible Hedingham, Great and Little Yeldham, with the consent of the Mortgagee, John Evans. The sale took place on 24th April 1883 at the Bell Inn, Castle Hedingham when the land occupied by William Corder was sold to Col. Arthur Swann Howard Lowe of Gosfield Hall. He also purchased more land near Liston Hall Farm, Kings Field near Southey Green Farm, together with the freehold Beer House at Southey Green occupied by Alfred Marshall and the adjoining cottage occupied by Joseph Finch. (19) William Corder therefore became a tenant of Col. Lowe and upon his death in 1888 of Arthur Courtauld Willoughby Lowe. William Corder occupied this land until he relinquished it in 1895. Whilst in William Corder's occupation the 10 acres comprised of three fields namely West Chandlers, Middle Chandlers and North Chandlers being field numbers 866, 867 and 868 respectively, with two smaller areas of land namely 865 and 868A. (Earlier, circa 1840's, plot 865 contained a dwelling with garden occupied by William Boreham (20) but by the 1870's this dwelling had disappeared). The five areas of land became one field named *"Chandler's Field"* by 1897. It remained in the ownership of the Lowe family until 1945, when it was sold following the death of George Hurst Armerin Lowe. A bungalow appropriately named *"Chandlers"* stands on the northern corner of this field south east of the former brickworks. Alfred William Worsfold was granted planning permission for this bungalow on his smallholding in November 1954. It was in the eastern corner of Chandlers Field that one of the medieval pottery kilns was found.

When William Corder took over the brickworks and pottery in 1859 there was one dwelling on the site which he occupied. According to earlier maps (21) it appeared to face the road. Sometime prior to 1876 William built a pair of red brick and tiled houses, with materials made on site, including ornate chimney pots. These no doubt advertised his craft as a brick & tile maker and potter. These houses were built at right angles to the road and slightly in front of the original house, which was demolished. These houses now known as 'Sunnyside' and 'South View' are still standing, although extended and much altered being rendered over, but the ornate chimney pots survive. William occupied one house with his family and his parents, John and Susan Corder occupied the other. Following John's death in 1880, William's elder brother, Robert Corder (1833-1915) and his family went into occupation when Robert was employed as a brickmaker by his brother. When Robert and Harriet Corder and their family returned to live at Crouch Green, Castle Hedingham during the 1880s the house was then rented to William

Cooke who was formerly master of the National School at Sible Hedingham. He had previously occupied the master's house attached to the school until he retired. After his death, his daughter, Miss. Constance Cooke, a piano and music teacher, continued to occupy the house.

On 13th June 1890 an unusual event took place at the house of William Corder. This was an inquest into the death of Golden Ernest Smith, aged 19 years, who drowned in a pond at Clay Hall Farm. A thirteen man jury was sworn in and after hearing evidence from witnesses the jury returned a verdict of *"Accidental Death"*. The jury included William Willett (1833-1913), a veteran of the Crimean War, and an uncle of Mrs. Alice Ann Corder (1861-1927), a daughter in law of William Corder. In addition to the Coroner there was also present a Doctor, Police Constable and other witnesses. It is interesting to note that the house was large enough to hold the hearing of an inquest. (22)

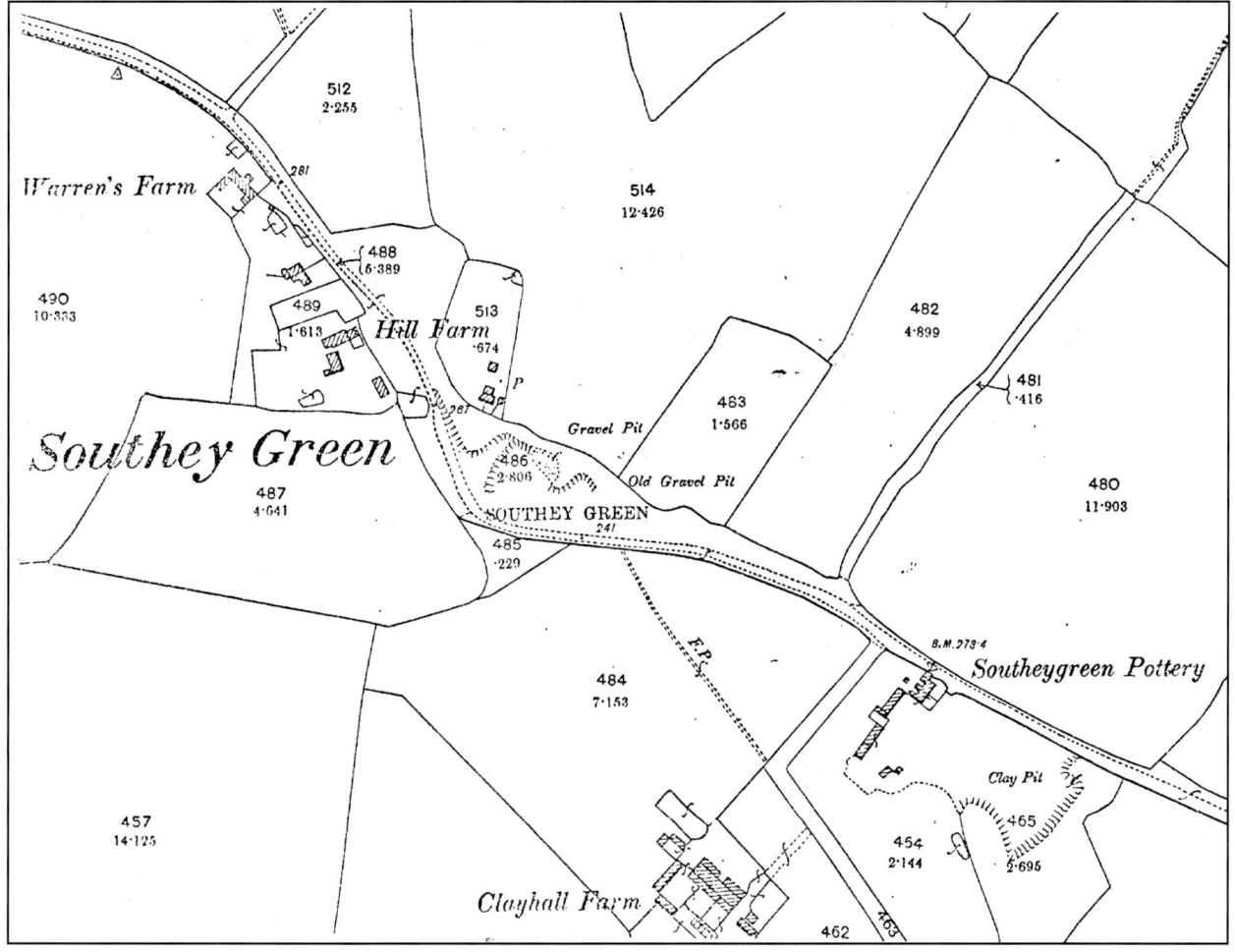

Southey Green Brick, Tile and Pottery Works and two houses from the 1897 Ordnance Survey map of scale 25 inches to one mile. In 1897 the Pottery, Clay and Gravel Pits were in the possession of William Corder: he previously occupied Warrens Farm on the left of the map.

Although William Corder took possession of the Southey Green Brickworks and Pottery in 1859 and at that time acquired the majority of it, it was not until 30th March 1870 that the remaining part, which was copyhold, was absolutely surrendered to him. He paid £100 for the purchase of the hereditaments on part of Southey Green extending to about 12 roods in length together with the tenement thereon and the brick kiln near or adjoining the premises. On 12th August 1870 William paid the sum of £33 1s 10d for an Award of Enfranchisement. The Lord of the Manor of Prayors in Sible Hedingham namely Lewis Ashurst Majendie of Hedingham Castle, Castle Hedingham, consented to the enfranchisement of the copyhold land and appurtenances held by William; namely the 12 roods in length and the tenement thereon. (23)

William owned the property until 24th November 1884 when he sold it for £345 0s 0d to Col. Arthur Swann Howard Lowe of Gosfield Hall, Gosfield. William then rented the property back from Col. Lowe who died on 12th August 1888. Probate of his estate was granted to Arthur Courtauld Willoughby Lowe who became owner of the property and upon his death it passed to George Hurst Armerin Lowe. William and later his son Harry Corder were therefore tenants of the Lowe family until 1942. When the Executors of George Lowe sold the Brickyard and two cottages in 1945 the property extended to 4a 2r 34p and the title commenced with a Conveyance on Sale dated 24th November 1884 when William Corder was the vendor. Interestingly, Warrens Farm was also owned by G.H.A. Lowe and in 1943 extended to 16a 3r 17p. The Lowe family's Southey Green Estate comprised of Warrens Farm, the Brickyard and two cottages, Chandlers Field, the Beer House and cottage together with Pevors and Perryfields Farms (extending to another 108 acres). (24)

During the early 1890s William Corder became proprietor of two more brickworks, at Potters Hall, Great Yeldham and at Park Hall Road, Gosfield. (see Chapters 7 and 8).

Warrens Farm, Chandlers Field and the brickworks at Gosfield were disposed of in 1895 as a result of the unfortunate bankruptcy of William Corder that year. This was caused by a number of reasons including the loss of horses, increase in coal prices during a coal strike, poor return from farming during the previous couple of years, heavy interest on money borrowed, customers who had defaulted in paying for goods supplied and the particular failure and lack of production at the Gosfield Brick Works. A large quantity of bricks, were supplied to a customer in London who failed to make payment. As a result of relinquishing Warrens Farm, Chandlers Field and the brickworks at Gosfield and selling plant, equipment, stock in trade and crops, substantial funds were raised to enable dividends to be made to creditors. In January 1896 William successively applied for his discharge in bankruptcy, which was granted, suspended for two years. (25) During this time the brickworks at Southey Green and Potters Hall continued to operate.

On 25th September 1896 Harry Corder (1873-1942) attended a meeting of the Halstead Union Assessment Committee at the Union House, Halstead and objected to the assessment of Southey Green Brick Field as being too high and the committee having considered the objections decided to reduce the assessment to £4 0s 0d gross and £3 10s 0d rateable value. (26) In about 1898 the brickworks at Potters Hall was sold to Charles Bocking.

William supplied bricks from his Southey Green Brick Works for building the former Martin's bakers shop and house at the junction of School Road, Church Street and Alexandra Road, Sible Hedingham. It was originally listed under Church Street but later in School Road. The shop and house was owned and occupied by members of the Martin family including Herbert Henry Martin who was a master baker. The bakery and shop closed in 1952 when it was incorporated into the house. (27) This was one of many buildings for which William Corder supplied bricks and other building materials.

The former Martin's bakers shop and house constructed circa 1880 with 'Hedingham reds' supplied by William Corder.

During Summer 1899 he supplied the pamments (the large floor bricks) for the tower floor and side aisles of Sible Hedingham Church when extensive restoration work was carried out to the west end of the building. The work included lowering and repaving the floors, the cost being met by the Misses Webster (see Chapter 19) and the Rev. Henry Warburton (28).

William Corder died in his home at Southey Green on 5th May 1903 aged 68 years. He was buried on 9th May 1903 in the Castle Hedingham Chapel Burial Ground (at the rear of the Congregational Chapel as it then was). (29) His son, Harry then became proprietor of the Southey Green Brick, Tile and Pottery Works.

A chimney pot made by William Corder at Southey Green Brick, Tile and Pottery Works. It stands 2 foot 6 inches high and is 13 inches in diameter. The ornate decoration around the shaft was formed with an incised roller being an instrument similar to a pastry wheel. It was applied while the pot was revolving on the potter's wheel and impressed a repeat or running pattern.

Some of the chimney pots made by William Corder were stamped around the shaft with his name. This particular chimney pot was removed from a chimney stack at Washlands Farm House, Sible Hedingham during the 1960s having been in use for over seventy years.

Chapter 4

HARRY CORDER (1873-1942) & SOUTHEY GREEN BRICK TILE AND POTTERY WORKS

Harry Corder was born 1st December 1873 at Southey Green, Sible Hedingham, a son of William Corder (1835-1903) by his second wife Eliza Corder formerly Eliza Downs (1842-1920). Harry was baptised on 31st May 1874 at Gestingthorpe Church.

At a young age, Harry followed his father and grandfather into the brick, tile and pottery industry and he eventually specialised in making pipes and pottery. In 1903 he succeeded his father as proprietor of the Southey Green Brick, Tile and Pottery Works and thereby became a master brickmaker and potter.

The Brick, Tile and Pottery Works at Southey Green immediately prior to the First World War showing two houses built by William Corder. Left to right: William Bruty, Fred, John and Harry Corder (three brothers), Henry and John Corder (cousins). This view shows the top of the kiln bottom left and the variety of pottery, pipes, bricks and tiles made.

Caroline Corder (1871-1951) at Southey Green prior to the First World War in front of the large shed used as stables and for pipemaking. The small shed on the left was the harness shed, when horses were used to deliver the products manufactured here.

Throughout the period 1885 to the Second World War there were a number of other brickworks operating in the Hedinghams. These brickworks principally made bricks, including many designs of ornamental bricks. They rarely made tiles, drain pipes or pottery. Therefore the Corder family at Southey Green concentrated on making different types of roofing tiles, various sizes of land drainage pipes, numerous types and shapes of chimney pots, flower pots and pamments. The reasons that tiles were the main product was that there was little or no competition from other brickworks, tiles required less clay than bricks, they were lighter to handle and quicker to burn. They were more expensive to buy because the clay required more preparation than for bricks. The clay at Southey Green, like that at Gestingthorpe, was very suitable for tiles, pottery and pipes, whereas at many of the other Hedingham brickworks the clay was not suitable for these products.

For much of the time only one brickmaker was employed at Southey Green who made sufficient bricks to facilitate loading the kiln. During the Edwardian era, white bricks as well as red bricks were made, (1) which was achieved by using a mixture of chalk and clay. The pipes were principally made by Harry Corder on a pipe machine which could be set to produce pipes of 2, 2.5, 3 or 4 inch diameter of any length. In addition the machine could be converted to produce ridge tiles of various measurements. The tiles manufactured included corrugated, pan, plain, ridge, hip, valley, eave, strip and nib tiles. Some pan tiles were glazed to form an impervious coating on the surface. Another tile was a one and a half plain tile which could be used as it was, or split into an ordinary plain tile and a half tile for use on the edges of roofs.

A selection of land drainage tiles and pipes

Left to right: Flat drain tile bottom with separate arch shaped drain tile top (sometimes called inverted V pipe and flat sole).

Flat drain tile bottom with separate semi circular drain tile top.

A combination of a drain top and bottom in one unit but still with a flat bottom.

A horse shoe shaped drainage pipe often called a Donkey-shoe pipe or tile.

Small circular drainage pipe.

Medium circular drainage pipe.

Large circular socket drainage pipe with a socket to facilitate attachment.

The above land drainage tiles and pipes were all made in the Hedingham and Gestingthorpe area and belong to the coarsest class of earthenware. Many were hand moulded flat and afterwards bent round a wooden core to the proper shape. Pipe making machines later superseded manual labour.

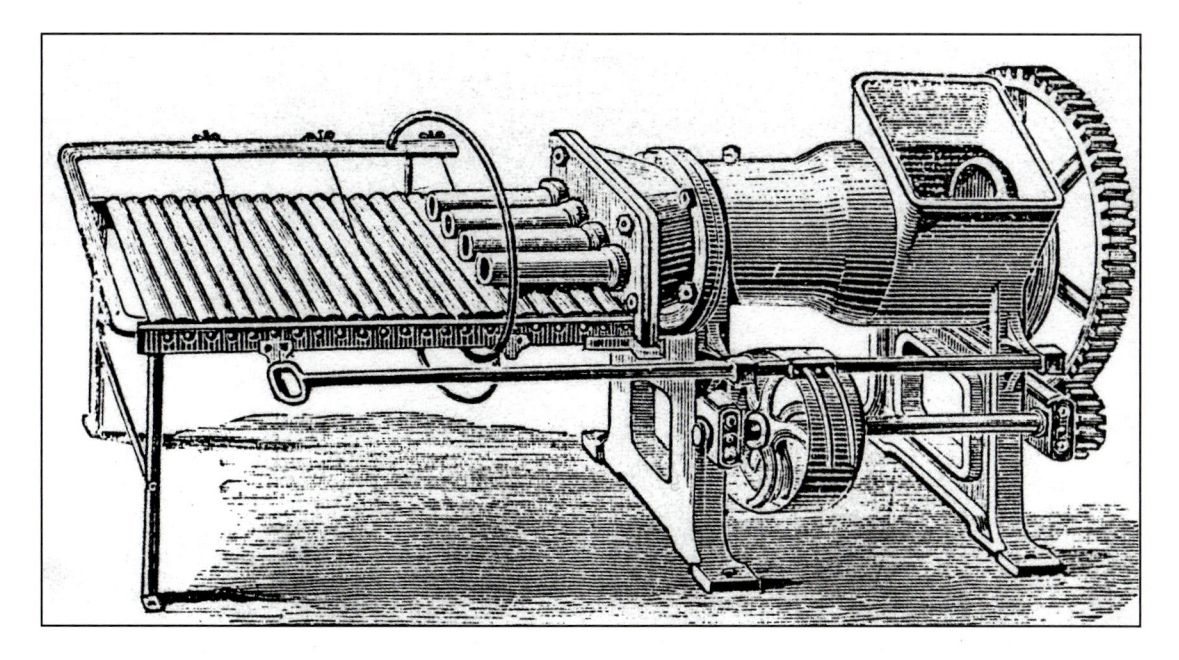

A pipe making machine, similar to that used at Southey Green illustrated in the British Clayworker, March 1918 p. 189. (Reproduced courtesy of The British Library Board). This extrusion machine combined the two processes of pugging and moulding at one time. It was easily stopped for cutting off the pipes and started again by means of a handle at the side of the cutting table. The machine at Southey Green had the added advantage of moulding ridge tiles using different fittings and dies.

A great variety of horticultural pots and earthenware kitchen pots, some glazed, were also made; some of which were very large and decorative. These included a number of three piece pedestals, the top section being a flower pot. A number of small flower pots, known as "thumb pots" were exported to Germany prior to the First World War. Among the large number of various types of chimney pots made at Southey Green were plain roll, roll base, beehive, curved roll, plain roll taper, moulded roll, round spiked, fluted top and many other types of plain round and ornamental round pots. In addition barrel tops were made as one piece with a comparatively small barrel on top and also in two pieces with a longer barrel top fitting inside the shaft of a curved roll or plain roll taper pot. Similar cowl tops were also made in one and two pieces. (2) The household earthenware manufactured included bread bins, pickling pans, milk pans and pitchers for dairies, seed pans and glazed dishes. Glazing was achieved with the addition of salt or lead, not only for some household earthenware but also for some drain pipes and pan tiles. The use of lead clays at Southey Green is evidenced by the sale of John Corder's stock of lead clay to Edward Bingham in 1880.

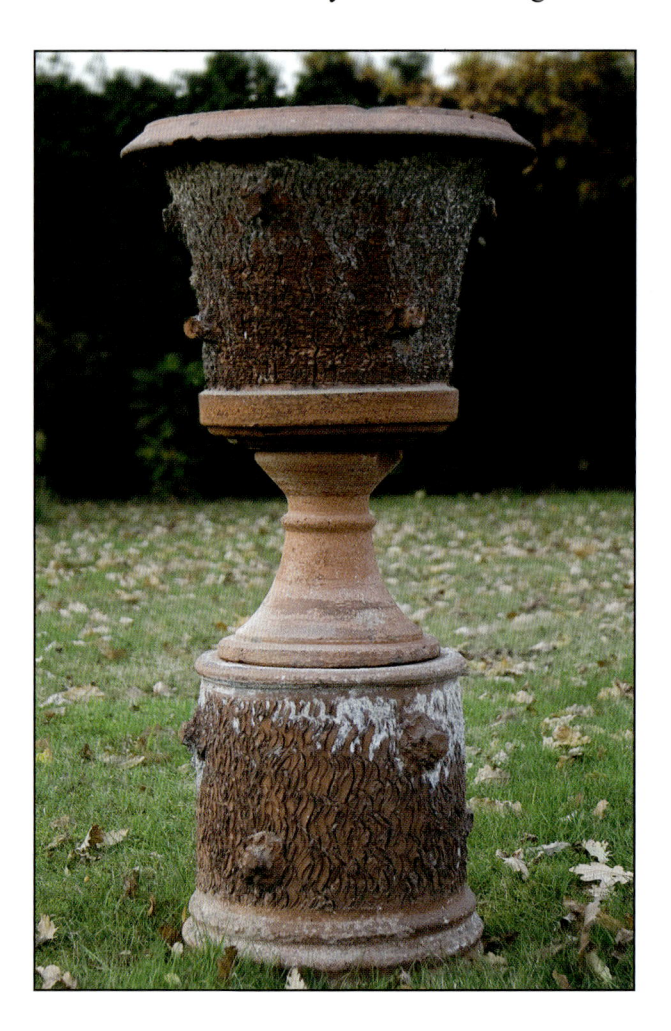

A flower pot made by Harry Corder during the early 1900s in three sections with a pedestal at the base, supporting a central pillar, surmounted by the flower pot. The pedestal and flower pot are imitation tree trunks each about one foot high with the flower pot about 20 inches in diameter. The central pillar is about 9 inches high making the complete set about 2 foot 9 inches in height. A large number of these were made and a couple can be seen in the photograph on page 35.

Fred Corder (1885-1961) left and his brother Harry Corder (1873-1942) right standing in front of the up-draught kiln at Southey Green circa 1931. The view shows the lean-to, with a mixture of corrugated and pan tile roof, which was used to store coal and provide shelter during firing. Harry always wore a straw hat in summer and a bowler hat in winter, even whilst at work in the brickyard.

The Land Value Duty Survey under The Finance Act 1910 shows that Harry Corder occupied the following property at Southey Green:-

Orchard and Brick Kiln   2a 2r 0p
House and Garden   1r 14p
Land   2a 0r 0p
Total   4a 3r 14p *with a gross value of £482.* (3)

During the First World War Harry Corder served in the National Reserve, later the Royal Defence Corps. He was not required to serve overseas but undertook home defence duties, due to his age and having a business to run. However as the First World War progressed he gradually lost his employees who went on active service overseas. At the outbreak of war in 1914 he employed six men. This number decreased to four in 1915 and to one in February 1916, namely his cousin, Henry Corder (1850-1934). With the workforce decimated it was a struggle for the business to operate with only Harry and Henry Corder between 1916 and 1918. The lighting restrictions contained in The Lighting Order of 22nd July 1916 caused trouble and inconvenience with regard to direct light from the kiln.

One employee, William George Bruty, whose family lived at Southey Green was killed in action on 3rd September 1916 aged 23 years. He was a Rifleman in the 14th Battalion, King's Royal Rifle Corps and was buried in Knightsbridge Cemetery, Somme, France. (4) John, Walter and Percy Corder also served as Riflemen in the King's Royal Rifle Corps and all three were badly injured at various times. Fred Corder served successively in the Essex Regiment, the Machine Gun Corps, the Royal Fusiliers and the Royal West Kent (Queen's Own) Regiment and was seriously injured at Ypres.

In Spring 1919, the brickworks and pottery returned to almost full strength when John, Fred and Walter Corder were discharged from the army and returned to civilian life. They all returned wounded or disabled in some way. Unfortunately John Corder could only carry out light work because of his injuries and the effects of the war and he died in 1922 at the age of 46 years. The return to peace brought hard times with the market, transportation and situations all changed. Handmade products gradually became uncompetitive in a national market, but production continued for another twenty years.

On 19th May 1924 the brickworks suffered severe damage when a terrific thunderstorm, unparalleled in living memory, broke out over north Essex. Considerable damage was done over a very large area from Sudbury, Bures, Halstead, Coggeshall to Gosfield and the Hedinghams. At Southey Green Brick Works, the drying sheds were flooded with storm water and several thousand 'green' tiles were spoilt through being saturated with water before being fired. A field of beans belonging to Harry Corder was also badly cut about. (5) This field, called "Lightfoots field", which contained an inexhaustible supply of good brick earth, which was never used, was opposite the brickworks adjacent to "Corder's Chase", which is the Green Lane or Right of Way from Southey Green to the village of Sible Hedingham. The field (no. 480 on the 1897 and 1923 25 inch Ordnance Survey maps) was nearly 12 acres in area.

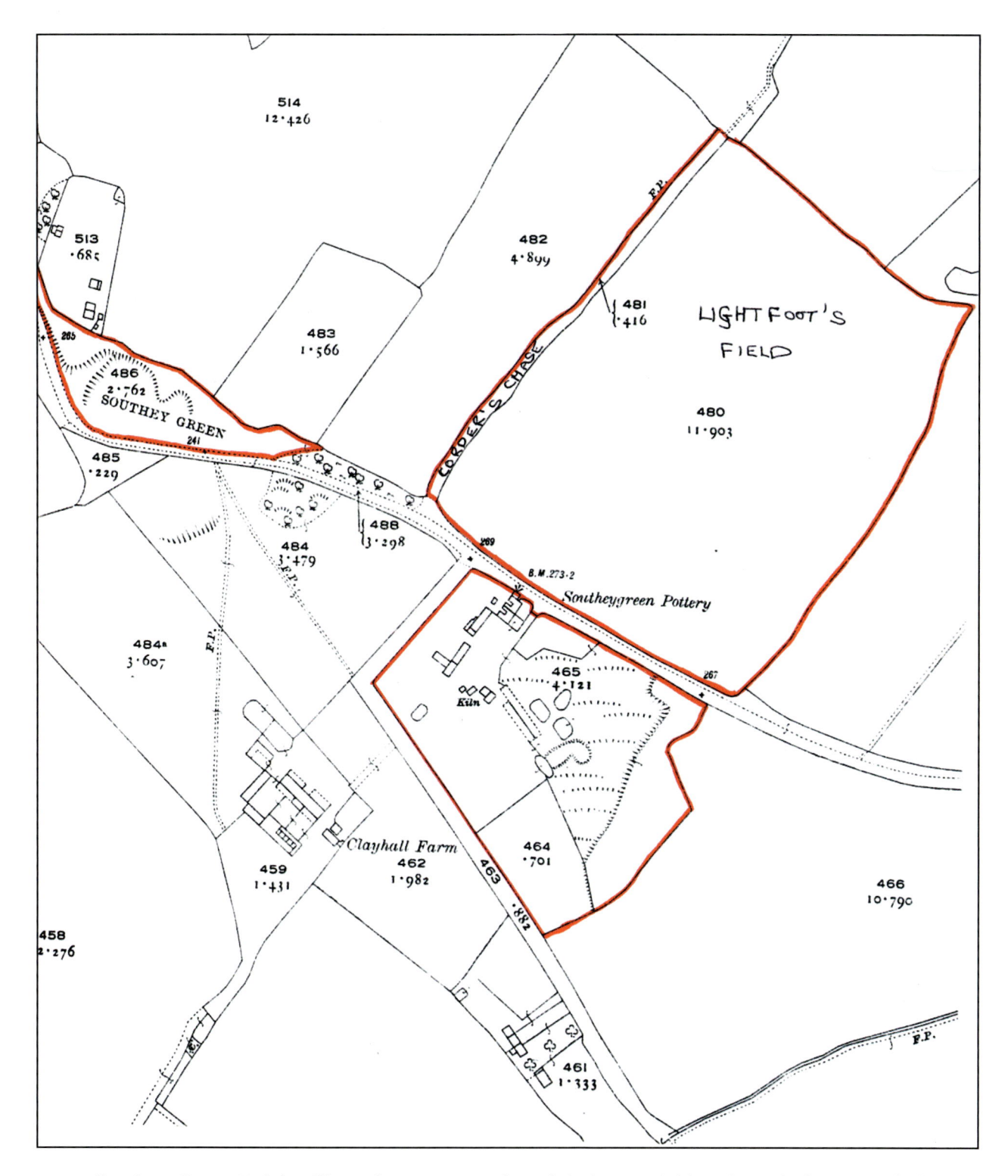

Southey Green Brick, Tile and Pottery Works, Lightfoot's Field and Sand Pits, occupied by Harry Corder edged red; from the Ordnance Survey Map 1923.

It was not until 1924 that a telegraphic line was erected from Braintree Corner via Starlings Hill, The Brickyard, Corder's Chase and the Village Green to a point near Southey Green Farm. The brickworks then had a telephone with the number Hedingham 15, which later changed to Hedingham 78.

Corder's Chase (designated as footpath number 65) viewed from Southey Green looking towards Sible Hedingham, was used by employees of the brickworks who lived in the village.

It is known that Harry Corder supplied bricks and tiles for the following:
1. 3,000 plain tiles and 100 eave tiles supplied to James Fletcher, market gardener of Sible Hedingham in August 1918. (6)
2. The roofing tiles for the twenty Council Houses in Alexandra Road, Sible Hedingham for the former Halstead Rural District Council during the summer of 1921. (Although Harry Corder did not supply the bricks, it is interesting to note that at a meeting of Halstead R.D.C. held in April 1921 that concern was expressed that these houses, which were being built by James S. Norton, a Halstead builder, were not being built with red facing bricks as previously planned. It was reported that the Housing Commissioner had cut out red bricks which cost 136/- a thousand against 55/- a thousand for those used but the bricks would be stuccoed - faced with plaster). (7)
3. Over 2,000 red bricks, including 25 x 2 inch bricks for the foundations and chimney of the mainly wooden bungalow of Woodview, Cut Maple, Sible Hedingham supplied from July to September 1928 for Maurice Springett. (8)
4. Tiles for the bungalow at Pleasant View, Braintree Corner, Sible Hedingham for James Gatwood.

5. Tiles for the two bungalows, now 136 and 138 Swan Street, Sible Hedingham, which were built by Percy James Parr, a builder of Castle Hedingham, for whom Bert Corder, a carpenter and joiner of Sible Hedingham, carried out the woodwork.

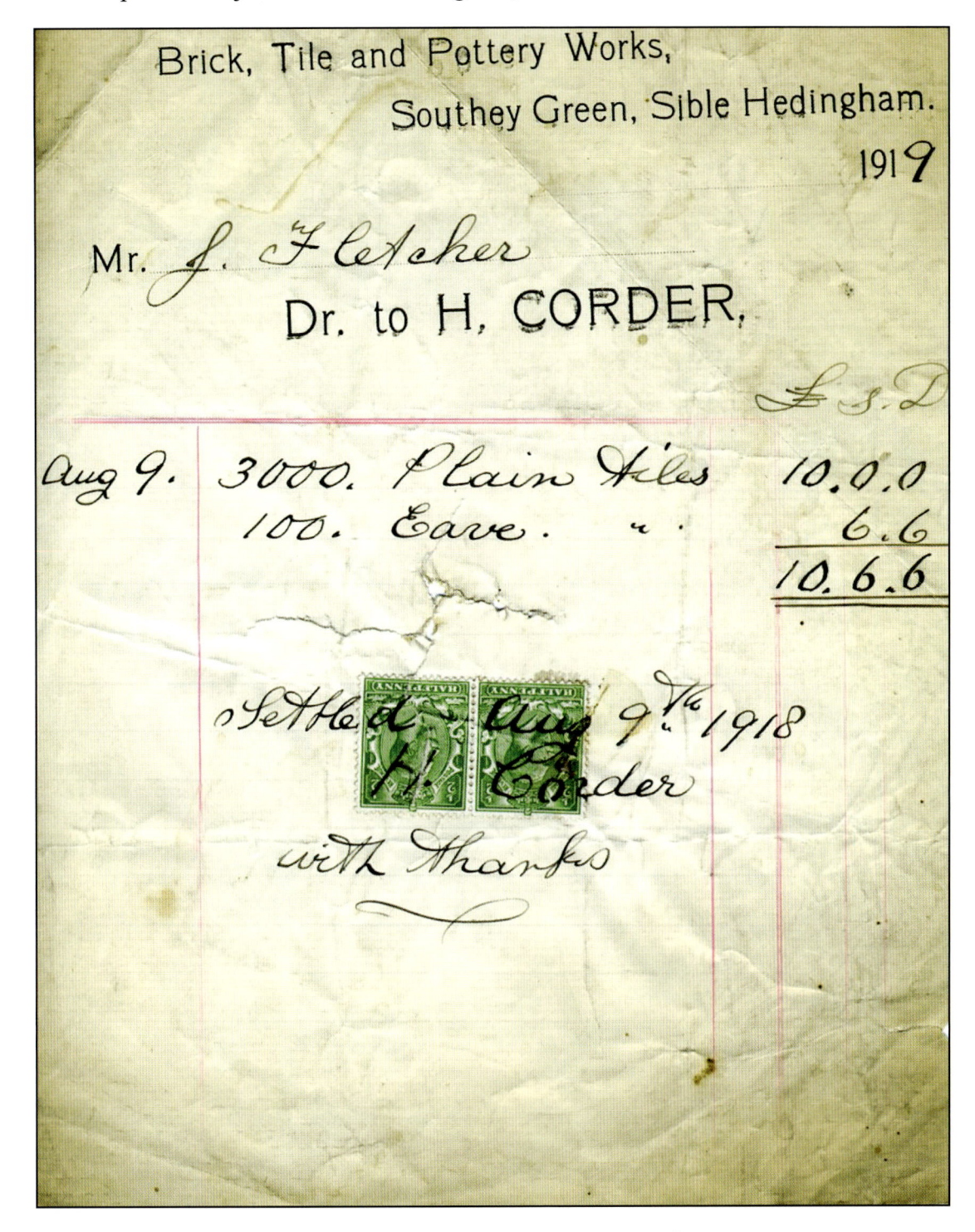

> Brick, Tile and Pottery Works,
> Southey Green, Sible Hedingham.
> 1919
>
> Mr. J. Fletcher
> Dr. to H. CORDER,
>
> £ s. d.
>
> Aug 9.   3000. Plain Tiles   10. 0. 0
>   100. Eave.   "   6. 6
>   10. 6. 6
>
> Settled Aug 9th 1918
> H. Corder
> with Thanks

Account to James Fletcher for tiles supplied on 9th August 1918

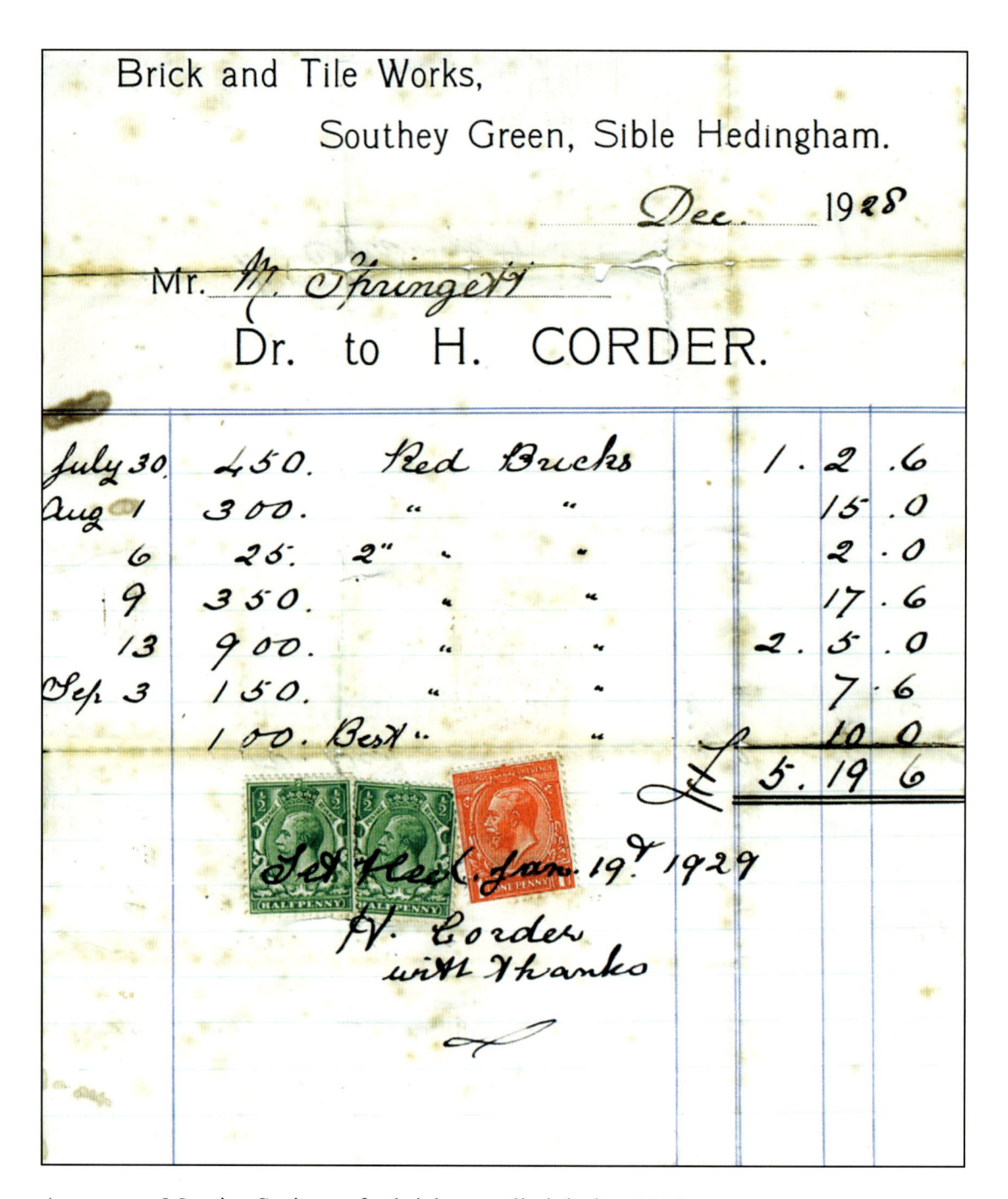

```
Brick and Tile Works,
    Southey Green, Sible Hedingham.
                                    Dec.    1928

Mr. M. Springett
        Dr. to  H. CORDER.
```

July 30	450.	Red Bricks		1	2	6
Aug 1	300.	"	"		15	0
6	25.	2" "	"		2	0
9	350.	"	"		17	6
13	900.	"	"	2	5	0
Sep 3	150.	"	"		7	6
	100. Best	"	"		10	0
			£	5	19	6

Settled Jan. 19th 1929
H. Corder
with thanks

Account to Maurice Springett for bricks supplied during 1928

Several local builders were among Harry Corder's regular customers including the following:
   Benjamin Bocking, Castle Hedingham.
   Messrs. Robert Bocking senior and Robert Bocking junior, Little Maplestead
   Harold Bragg, Halstead
   Bert William Corder, Sible Hedingham
   George Thomas Elsdon, Sible Hedingham
   (Arthur) Frank Gibson, Sible Hedingham
   Messrs. Palmer and Corder, Sible Hedingham

James Smith Norton, Halstead (also a builders merchant including tiles)
Percy James Parr, Castle Hedingham
George Sharp, Halstead

Harry Rippingale, haulage contractor of Gestingthorpe (see chapter 17) occasionally carried out haulage work for Messrs. Palmer and Corder of Sible Hedingham and for Messrs. Bocking of Little Maplestead. For example on 16th July 1930, 2000 tiles were delivered to Bishop's Stortford for Messrs. Palmer and Corder at a cost of £1 15s 0d. On 28th October 1930 chimney pots (and other building materials) were delivered to Wickham St. Paul for Messrs. Bocking at a cost of 5s 0d (9). The chimney pots made at Southey Green must have been sturdy because it is reputed that when Robert Bocking finished constructing a chimney he put his head on the top of each chimney pot and lifted his feet up in the air. Whilst this practise was potentially dangerous it is understood that he never fell or suffered any injury. Perhaps it was his way of testing the strength of chimneys and chimney pots?

The up-draught kiln being fired in 1937 with Harry Corder on top of the kiln and his brother Fred standing below. Harry was on top of the kiln to control the draught by opening and closing the gaps in the layer of old bricks, known as platting.

Apart from John, Fred, Henry and Walter Corder, other employees of Harry Corder at various times between 1903 and 1939 were a cousin, John Corder (1863-1957), Harry Willett (1869-1950) a tile maker of Sible Hedingham (and a brother in law of George Corder), Sidney Charles (Sid) Clark (born 1900) a tilemaker from Coggeshall, Robert (Bob) Earey a brickmaker of Sible Hedingham, Albert Finch (1909-1974) a tilemaker of Gestingthorpe and Harry Rulton, also known as Harry Harding, a general labourer of Sible Hedingham and later of Gosfield. Harry Rulton (born 1891) was first employed by Harry Corder prior to the First World War and in the 1911 census was described as a *'brickyard labourer'* aged 20 (10). Following service in the Essex Regiment during the First World War, he returned to his former employment with Harry Corder in 1919 and continued until 1939. The Rulton and Bruty families were neighbours at Southey Green for many years. In the 1930's Harry Corder paid his men double the wage of an agricultural worker. The work was skilled but seasonal, as in the winter months the men could only dig out clay for the following year, when they worked a fortnight on and a fortnight off, with none of the benefits available today. The only full time employee was Fred Corder.

A bird bath constructed by Albert Finch with bricks made by him at Southey Green circa late 1930s. Each brick measures about 2 inches by 1 inch by 1 inch and the bird bath is about 20 inches high and 10 inches square. It stood in his garden at Audley End, Gestingthorpe, for many years until his widow gave it to the author.

This earthenware model known as *'The Duck Girl'* was made by Albert Finch when employed by Harry Corder during the 1930s. Albert's widow Gladys, kindly gave it to the author some years ago.

The Southey Green Brick, Tile and Pottery Works was forced to close upon the outbreak of the Second World War in September 1939 because of the blackout regulations and the risk of the pilots of enemy aircraft seeing the fire from the up- draught kiln. The 'green' products remained on site until 1942 when they were transported to Bulmer Brick and Tile Works where they were successfully fired in their down-draught kiln. This operated during wartime as the fires could be adequately covered to prevent them being seen by enemy pilots.

Harry Corder died at his home at the Brickfield, Southey Green on 6th February 1942 and was buried in Castle Hedingham Cemetery. His brother, Fred Corder, as administrator of his estate, arranged for the contents of the brickworks to be sold by auction on 19th March 1942. The auctioneer was Jesse Quinton of Balls & Balls, who acted for the Corder family for many years, including as agent in the sale of Bay Cottage, Sible Hedingham in 1969. The solicitor was Ronald Long (later Sir Ronald Long) senior partner of Smith, Morton & Long who acted for the Corder family for over fifty years.

> **THE BRICKYARD, SOUTHEY GREEN, SIBLE HEDINGHAM.**
>
> ### BALLS and BALLS
>
> Have been favoured with instructions from the Exors. of the late Mr. H. Corder, to Sell by Auction, on THURSDAY, MARCH 19th, 1942, at 1.30 o'clock,
>
> ## STOCK AND UTENSILS IN TRADE
>
> ### OF A BRICKMAKER,
>
> Comprising: Hake Covers, Tile Boards, 10 Barrows, Tile Trays, Tile Cover, Wheeling Plates, Forge, Anvil, Scales and Weights.
>
> ### THE LARGE STOCK OF VARIOUS BRICKS AND TILES,
>
> Pamments, Flower Pots and Drainpipes.
>
> ### THE MACHINERY AND EQUIPMENT
> Including:
>
> 6-h.p. "Petter" Oil Engine, 6-h.p. "Lister" Petrol Engine, 2¼-h.p. Petrol Engine, Pipe-making Machine, Saw Bench, Pug Mills.
>
> Quantity of Grass Hay.
>
> 10-h.p. STANDARD SALOON MOTOR-CAR and other effects.
>
> Catalogues may be had of the Auctioneers, Castle Hedingham and Braintree, Essex.

> ### OUR DIARY OF COMING EVENTS.
> **March.**
> 19—Sale of Stock and Utensils in Trade of a Brickmaker, Southey Green, Sible Hedingham, by Messrs. Balls and Balls, 1.30.

Notices of sale of stock and equipment from the Halstead Gazette of 6th March 1942.

The sale included a large stock of various bricks, tiles, pamments, flower-pots and drainpipes. The utensils in trade comprised of hack covers, tile boards, ten barrows, tile trays, tile covers, wheeling plates, forge, anvil, scales and weights. The machinery and equipment included a 6hp "Petter" oil engine, 6hp "Lister" petrol engine, 2.25hp petrol engine, pipe-making machine, saw bench and pug mills. There was also a quantity of grass hay, a 10hp Standard saloon motorcar and other effects. The guns were sold to Ernest Finch, landlord of the Half Moon Public House, Queen Street, Sible Hedingham. (11)

The majority of 'green' goods, loo boards, (12) a pug mill and many of the moulds were purchased by Lawrence Minter of the Bulmer Brick and Tile Company Limited. Following the auction several lorry loads of goods were transported from Southey Green to Bulmer. One load was so heavy that the lorry could not climb up Sudbury Hill, Castle Hedingham. Therefore half the goods were unloaded onto Forge Green, Castle Hedingham. Following unloading of half at Bulmer the lorry returned to collect the remaining goods from the Village Green.

BARTON & Co.,

STOUR VALLEY IRON WORKS, SUDBURY, SUFFOLK.

ENGINEERS, MILLWRIGHTS,

MAKERS OF

ALL KINDS OF BRICKFIELD MACHINERY.

Pug Mills, Wash Mills, Windlasses, Barrows, Brick Moulds, Groove Pulleys, Driving Chain, &c., &c.

Improved Pug-Mill and Windlass combined.

An advertisement from the British Clayworker of December 1898 (Reproduced courtesy of The British Library Board). Barton & Co made brickfield machinery for many brickworks in Essex and Suffolk including the pug mills used at Southey Green.

A Barton pug mill was purchased by Cyril Philp, a farmer and well known traction engine enthusiast of Kirby Hall, Castle Hedingham with the intention of converting it into a machine to wash sugar beet. This idea was not successful and in about 1973 this pug mill was acquired by William Martin, a Sible Hedingham builder, who used it when making bricks from clay left over at the former Sible Hedingham Red Brick Company works, which had closed during the 1950s. The bricks were made and fired at The Tythings, Rectory Meadow, Sible Hedingham and were the last bricks to be made in the Hedinghams and had the brick mark "WKM" in the frogs. Thereafter Bill Martin kindly gave the pug mill to the author who many years later passed it to Peter Minter (son of Lawrence Minter) who preserved it, with other brickmaking machinery, tools and moulds at Bulmer Brick and Tile Works.

Following the sale of Southey Green Brickyard in 1942 Caroline and Susan Corder, the two surviving sisters of Harry and Fred Corder, moved to Bay Cottage, Swan Street, Sible Hedingham where they made their home with Fred and Sarah Corder and their daughter Beatrice. The brick, tile and pottery industry at Southey Green came to an end after a period of over four hundred years and for over eighty years it was in the ownership of the Corder family.

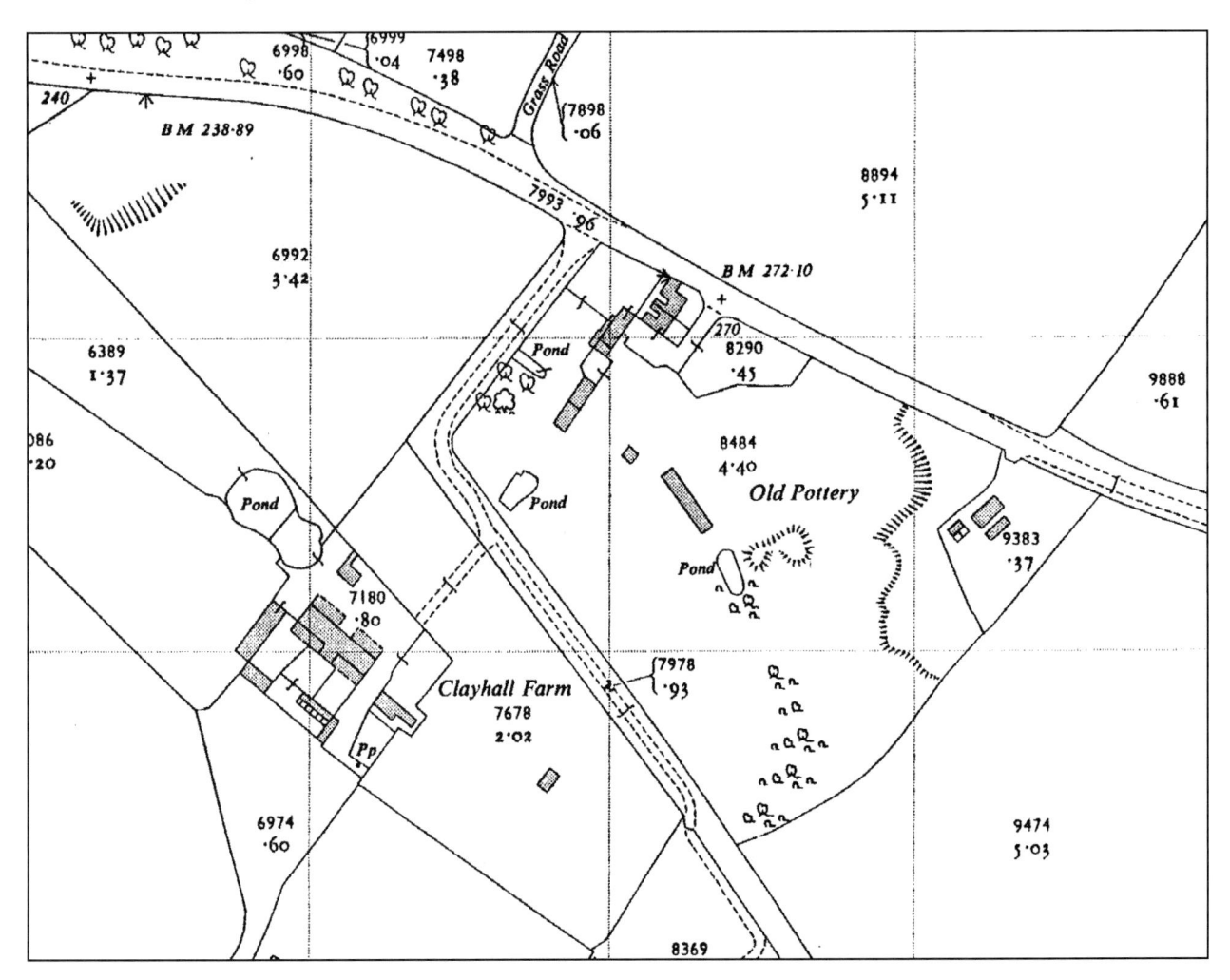

The 25 inch to one mile Ordnance Survey Map showing the remaining buildings of the former Pottery in 1953.

The following description of the former brickyard at Southey Green in circa 1958 is given by the author, Jack Lindsay, in his book, 'The Discovery of Britain':

> *"I have a look around Forrey Green and Southey Green. The Corder works are in decay. The clay has been dug from around the mouldering furnace and drying shed - the brick sheds, long and red-tiled, always have a pleasant look. A ploughman tells me about the things that Corder made, tiles and various building materials. 'He built those cottages ……….. There's some clay left, but not much"* (13)

The kiln and one of the long tile sheds remained on site until they were demolished in 1967. Another tile shed disappeared during the 1970s but the tack room, garage and pipe making shed remain in use as stables. The site of the brickyard and clays pits is now used as a paddock for horses and the two red brick houses built by William Corder remain.

Two of the surviving buildings at Southey Green in 1967. The building on the left was a former tile making and drying shed, which was later demolished. The building on the right was the barn, tack room, garage and pipe making shed, where the pipe making machine was housed and land drainage pipes and ridge tiles were made. This is the same building which appears on the photograph on page 36.

The remains of the kiln in 1967 when almost demolished

A former tile making and drying shed in 1967, shortly before it was demolished. There were originally two of these long sheds with pan tiled roofs.

Chapter 5

JOHN CORDER (1876-1922)

John Corder was born 23rd May 1876 at Southey Green Pottery, Sible Hedingham, a son of William and Eliza Corder and was baptised on 27th May 1877 at Gestingthorpe Church. When old enough he followed his father into the brickmaking and pottery industry at Southey Green.

John Corder whilst serving as a rifleman in the Kings Royal Rifle Corps during the First World War

In the 1891 census (1) John is recorded as a Flower Pot Maker at the age of 14 years. In both the 1901 census (2) and the 1911 census (3) he is recorded as a brickmaker. He was employed by his father until 1903 and thereafter by his elder brother, Harry Corder. It was heavy work being a brickmaker. A standard 'green' brick weighed 10lbs when made and a load of 30 bricks on a cradle barrow therefore weighed about 300lbs. To keep the balance of these large and long one wheeled barrows was not easy. As each brick had to be handled at least twice a brickmaker could shift some four tons of clay a day. Some of the specials, such as coping bricks, can weigh as much as one hundredweight each when 'green'.

John volunteered for service in the First World War and joined the Kings Royal Rifle Corps in November 1915. He served in France as a Rifleman and according to his obituary had many thrilling experiences. On one occasion he was buried, with others, in a blown up trench, he was also gassed and suffered badly from its effects. (4) As a result of his wounds caused by military service he was disabled and honourably discharged on 2nd November 1918, a few days before the Armistice. He received the Silver War Badge and a Certificate in recognition of his honourable discharge as well as the British War and Victory Medals.

A lion made at Southey Green Brick, Tile and Pottery Works by John Corder.

The effects of the war prevented him from continuing the heavy work of a brickmaker and he therefore looked after his own poultry, which he kept at Southey Green Brickyard and Pottery and was able to make a living selling eggs. He also carried out some light gardening work and sold garden produce including fruit and vegetables.

The garden at Southey Green Brick, Tile and Pottery Works circa 1931 photographed from a first floor window of the house when occupied by Harry Corder and his sisters, Caroline and Susan Corder. The road from Cut Maple to Southey Green was behind the hedge on the left. During the Victorian era the garden area was part of the brickyard before it expanded further away and the garden was created. It was in this garden that John carried out light work after the First World War.

Although he became practically an invalid and did not enjoy good health he was most patient and cheerful. He suffered considerably from his injuries and the effects of the war, in particular gassing, resulting in his death at his home at Southey Green on 13th July 1922 aged 46 years. (4) He was one of the last to be buried in the Chapel Burial Ground at the rear of the Congregational Chapel (now the URC) in Castle Hedingham, where his parents and grandparents were also buried.

A selection of roofing tiles found in the Hedingham area similar to those made by the Corder family at Southey Green and their other works at Gosfield and Great Yeldham.
Left to right back row:
A plain tile with two holes in it for the reception of tile-pins, by which it was hung on wooden laths. (Later plain tiles were made with a couple of nibs at the head of the tile to hang over the laths).
A corrugated pan tile.
Left to right front row:
A pan tile showing the under side with a nib.
A hip tile for the external projection or ridge where two portions of a roof meet at an angle. (Conversely valley tiles were used if the angle is towards the inside of the building forming a gutter).
A glazed pan tile, with its impervious coating on the surface.

Chapter 6

FRED CORDER (1885-1961)

Fred Corder was born 17th January 1885 at The Pottery, Southey Green, Sible Hedingham, the youngest son of William and Eliza Corder and was baptised 11th March 1885 at Sible Hedingham Church.

Fred Corder at Southey Green Brick, Tile and Pottery Works in 1931.

He followed his father and elder brothers into the brick and tile making industry. He is recorded on the 1901 census (1) as a *'tile maker'* when he was employed by his father. From 1903 to 1939, with the exception of First World War service, he was employed by his elder brother, Harry Corder. Fred is recorded on the 1911 census (2) as a *'Brick Carter'*.

He used horses and a cart to deliver bricks, tiles, pipes and pottery and to collect orders. He took quantities of pottery to sell at local markets such as at Sudbury, Suffolk. At the end of the day if Fred fell asleep in the cart, the horses found their way home to Southey Green from Sudbury and elsewhere. The horses and carts were owned by William and Harry Corder successively and stabled at Southey Green Brickyard and Pottery. Prior to the acquisition of engines, horses and ponies were also used to power the pug mills. Fred loved horses and throughout his life followed the East Essex Hunt, often with his cousin John Corder (1863-1957). As a young boy Fred sometimes failed to attend School and followed the hounds, unknown to his family and teachers.

When lorries came into wider use, customers were required to make their own transport arrangements for collection of products. The horses, carts and tack were then sold and Harry Corder purchased a motorbike, which he rode until a hand injury prevented him from continuing. He then purchased a new open top Morris Cowley Bullnose motor car with a *'dickey'* seat at the back and thereby owned one of the first six cars in Sible Hedingham. It was usually driven by his brother Fred Corder who held a full driving licence.

Fred Corder driving the Morris Cowley Bullnose motor car photographed outside the gates of Over Hall, Gestingthorpe, circa late 1920s. His passengers are Winifred Bristow, Edith Bristow and Beatrice Corder. Winifred and Edith were daughters of George and Edith Bristow formerly Downs. Edith Downs was Fred's first cousin.

The Morris Cowley Bullnose was replaced with a 10 horse power Standard Coventry saloon number BNO 451, which was registered new to Harry Corder on 14th July 1934. Fred Corder drove the Standard 10 until the petrol shortage caused by the Second World War. The car was then stored in its garage at Southey Green until it was sold with the remaining stock, machinery and equipment of the Brickyard in March 1942. Both cars were mainly used in connection with the Brick, Tile and Pottery business and only occasionally for private use.

Fred with the Standard Coventry outside his home, Swan Cottage, Swan Street, Sible Hedingham circa 1935.

Fred with his daughter Beatrice, Pedro a Golden Retriever gun dog and the Standard Coventry motor car at Southey Green, circa 1935. This view clearly shows that the pair of houses built by William Corder were constructed using Flemish bond brickwork. There is a stack of building materials for sale in the right background.

In 1916 Fred Corder enlisted into the army serving successively in the Essex Regiment, The Machine Gun Corps, the Royal Fusiliers and the Royal West Kent (Queen's Own) Regiment. In the First World War it was common practice to draft men in from other regiments in order to make up losses when heavy casualties were sustained. Fred was drafted from one regiment to another on three occasions, which was more than usual. With heavy casualties in his first three regiments he was clearly fortunate to have survived. In October 1917 his mother received notification from the Army Record Office stating that Fred, then of The Machine Gun Corps was suffering from gun shot wounds in the knee and arm of a severe nature. (3) He still had fragments of shrapnel in his body when he died in 1961.

After the First World War he resumed work for his brother at Southey Green Brickyard and Pottery principally as a tilemaker. He also fired the kiln at night, whilst Harry Corder fired it during the day. Whilst firing the kiln they occupied a hut adjacent to it. Firing the kiln was the most important and responsible position in every brickworks. A mistake could lead to heavy losses and much unnecessary work. The kiln at Southey Green was a square up draught kiln. Great care was taken with 'stacking' or 'setting' the dried products in the kiln to allow the heat to circulate evenly to fire them. Products were arranged with great skill and accurately spaced to provide suitable flow distribution of heat to give uniform temperature during firing. Two inch pipes were often stacked inside four inch pipes to save space. After the kiln was loaded the entrance was sealed up using a few courses of old bricks, which were temporarily daubed with clay paste or sand filling. Layers of old bricks were also placed over the top of the kiln to protect the dried bricks below. During the course of firing , Harry and Fred Corder opened and closed gaps between these old bricks to control the draught, known as platting. The kiln had two chambers, one above the other. The fire was in the lower chamber and the products were fired in the upper chamber. After loading and sealing the kiln, coal fires were gradually applied and the firing took between three and five days and nights. The products fired in up draught kilns burnt unevenly; the products near the bottom were well burnt and dark red in colour whilst those at the top were not so well burnt and were a lighter red. The products were usually stacked in three grades depending upon colour.

Upon the closure of the Southey Green Brickyard and Pottery, at the outbreak of the Second World War in September 1939, Fred obtained employment with Rippers Limited, joinery manufacturers in Hedingham, until his retirement in 1950. During the war he undertook fire watch duties at Rippers during the night, being used to night work with firing the kiln. The factory, which undertook important work to help the war effort, was a target and occasionally bombed.

In March 1942, Fred, as Administrator of the Estate of his late brother, Harry Corder, arranged for the sale of the Southey Green Brickyard and Pottery. At about this time he was invited to become Manager of a brickworks in Colchester but declined the offer. Fred died on 29th May 1961 at his home, Bay Cottage, Sible Hedingham aged 76 years and was buried in Sible Hedingham Churchyard on 1st June 1961.

Fred, his wife Sarah (1894-1981), with their daughter Beatrice (1925-2006) and Toby who was Harry Corder's gun dog at Southey Green Brick, Tile and Pottery Works on 12th August 1931.

Beatrice Corder with Pedro at Southey Green Brick, Tile and Pottery Works in 1935. In the background is a stack of plain tiles ready for sale

Beatrice with Pedro at Southey Green in 1935. In the background is a vertical pug mill, in the centre a movable drying shed and on the right a tile making and drying shed.

Chapter 7

POTTER'S HALL BRICK, TILE AND POTTERY WORKS, GREAT YELDHAM

The brickworks at Potter's Hall, Great Yeldham was started circa 1872 by Henry Edward Whitlock (1850-1913) when he lived at Grove House. The ancient name of Potter's Hall suggests that pottery may have been made on this site during an earlier period but no evidence of this has been found. Henry Whitlock was a member of the Whitlock family, who later became well known as agricultural engineers and manufacturers of earth moving equipment.

In 1884 George Hardy & Son succeeded Henry Whitlock as proprietors of the brickworks. George Hardy & Son were also builders in Great Yeldham and continued their building business after selling the brickworks to William Corder (1835-1903) in 1892. (1)

William Corder continued making a variety of bricks, tiles and drain pipes but also introduced the manufacture of pottery such as chimney pots. The brickworks had one kiln and was conveniently situated close to Great Yeldham Station on the Colne Valley and Halstead Railway, which had opened to Great Yeldham in 1862. William's nephew, Henry Corder (1850-1934) managed these brickworks for his uncle and lived in nearby Poole Street. (See chapter 14)

Henry Corder manager of Potters Hall Brick Works photographed in 1924.

William Corder is recorded as a brickmaker at Great Yeldham in the 1895 Directory of Essex. (1)   The 1896 Register of Electors for Great Yeldham records *'William Corder of Sible Hedingham'*, qualifying as an elector *'as occupier of buildings and brickyard at Potters Hall Brick Yard, Great Yeldham'*.

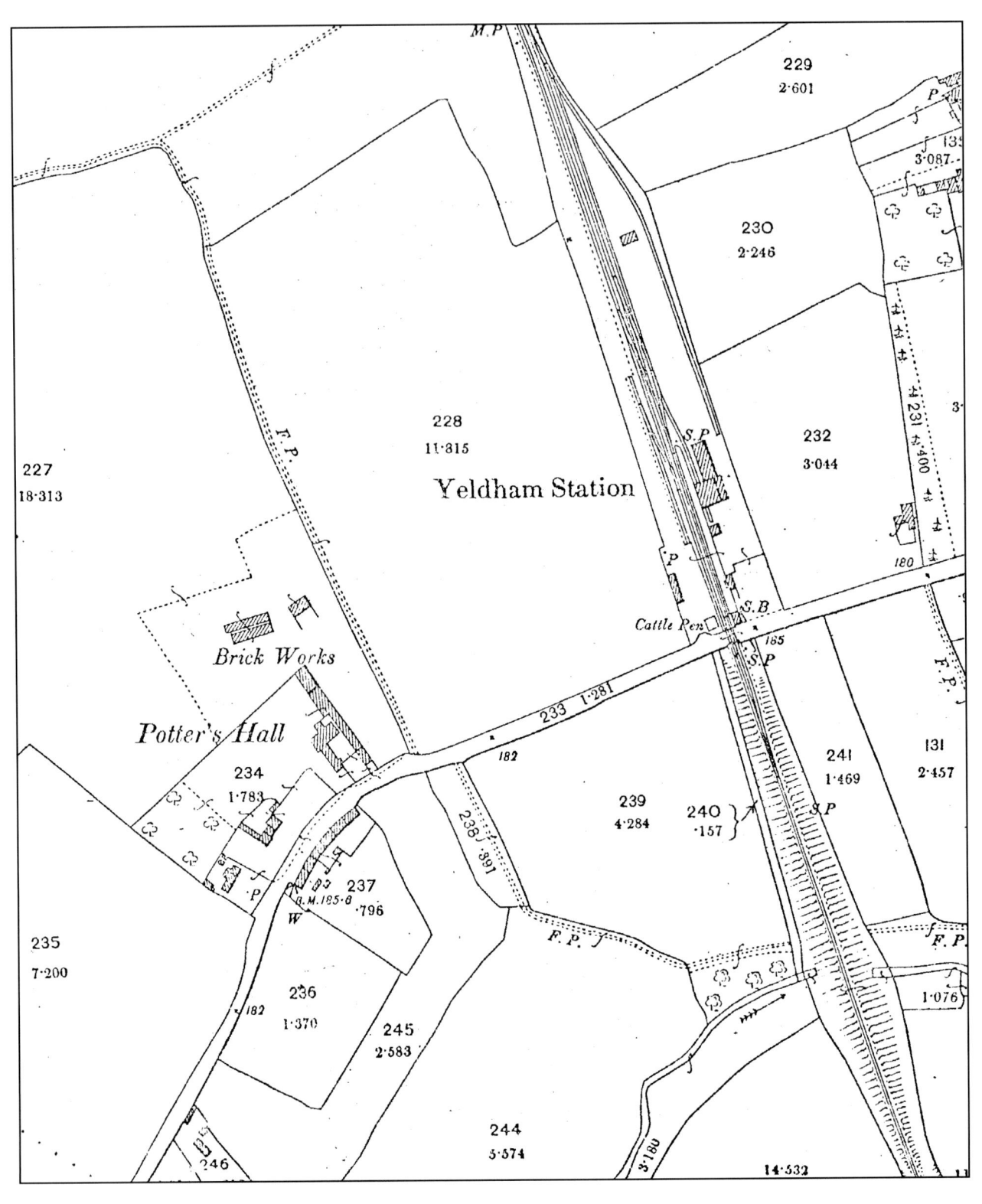

Potters Hall Brick Works in 1897 whilst in the possession of William Corder. Note the close proximity to Yeldham Railway Station to facilitate transportation.

The site of the brickworks was just under two acres. (2) The clay was dug on site at the rear of the brickworks and the old clay pit survived for many years before it was filled in. The remains of a number of mammals were found when clay was dug out of the clay pit in 1878 and again in 1896. The bones found in 1878 had been split open (possibly for their marrow?). Land and freshwater shells were also found but unfortunately all these finds were destroyed.   The discovery in February 1896 resulted in the finds being preserved in the Museum of Practical Geology, London. William Corder's employees discovered the remains whilst digging out clay for brickmaking.   Members of the Geological Survey visited the site on 5th March 1896 and inspected the remains in the hands of the workmen at the brickworks.   The experts detected many portions of the antlers and limb bones of Red Deer, some teeth of a Brown Bear, bones and portions of a lower jaw with grinding teeth of a Rhinoceros and part of the tooth of an Elephant.   There were also some foot bones and large grinding teeth of an Ox and the antler of a Roebuck. The remains of the Brown Bear and Roebuck in a Pleistocene bed in Essex were quite rare. (3)

The site of the former clay pits and brickyard is in the foreground of this photograph taken by the author in 1967. In the background are two cottages now known as Recreation Cottages, which was originally the granary for Potters Hall Farm. The two storied brick and tiled granary was converted for George Goodchild in 1929-30 by B. W. Corder builder and contractor of Sible Hedingham.

Potters Hall Farm buildings photographed by the author in 1967, were demolished two years later. They were built with bricks and pan tiles made at the adjacent brickyard.

In about 1898 the brickworks was purchased by Charles Bocking, who farmed Potters Hall Farm and was also a General Carter. The brickworks closed in 1908 and was advertised for sale with the following description:

> "............... there is also forming part of the property a BRICKYARD WITH KILN and range of Board and Pantile Drying Sheds and the land has the reputation of containing Good Brick Earth. Mr. Charles Bocking who claims to be paid by valuation for the Brick Drying Sheds, Kiln bars, doors and boards and other brickmaking plant; also for the pug mills, or to be at liberty to remove same before the end of his tenancy if he so elects." (4)

Throughout its existence, this brickworks manufactured both red and yellow/white bricks, which was unusual for a small brickworks. The red and yellow/white bricks contained brick marks in the frogs *"WHITLOCK YELDHAM"* and *"W.C."* for William Corder. Many of the reds were particularly dark in colour and Whitlock reds were used in the construction of the Whitlock Chaff Works at Poole Farm, Poole Street, Great Yeldham, which includes some particularly attractive moulded brickwork.

Chapter 8

PARK HALL ROAD BRICK WORKS, GOSFIELD

During the nineteenth century there were two brickworks on the north side of Park Hall Road, Gosfield. One, immediately north east of Easter Cottage, was in operation by 1845 until at least 1876. A century later the former brickmaker's cottage became the home of Phyllis Rayner, a descendant of the Rayner family of brickmakers and potters from Gestingthorpe. Easter Cottage is now the home of Richard and Joanne Beavis.

The other brickworks, north west of Park Hall Farm, on the Gosfield Hall Estate, was in operation intermittently during the second half of the nineteenth century. It had closed by 1876 when it was described as '*Old Brick Field*' but later re-opened. Its proprietor from 1890 to 1895 was William Corder (1835-1903). It was managed by his eldest son, George Corder (1863-1938) who then lived in a nearby house in Park Hall Road. It was here that his son Harry Corder (1891-1906) was born. The brickworks extended to 3.316 acres including one kiln, various brickmaking and drying sheds, a water pump and clay pits. (1)

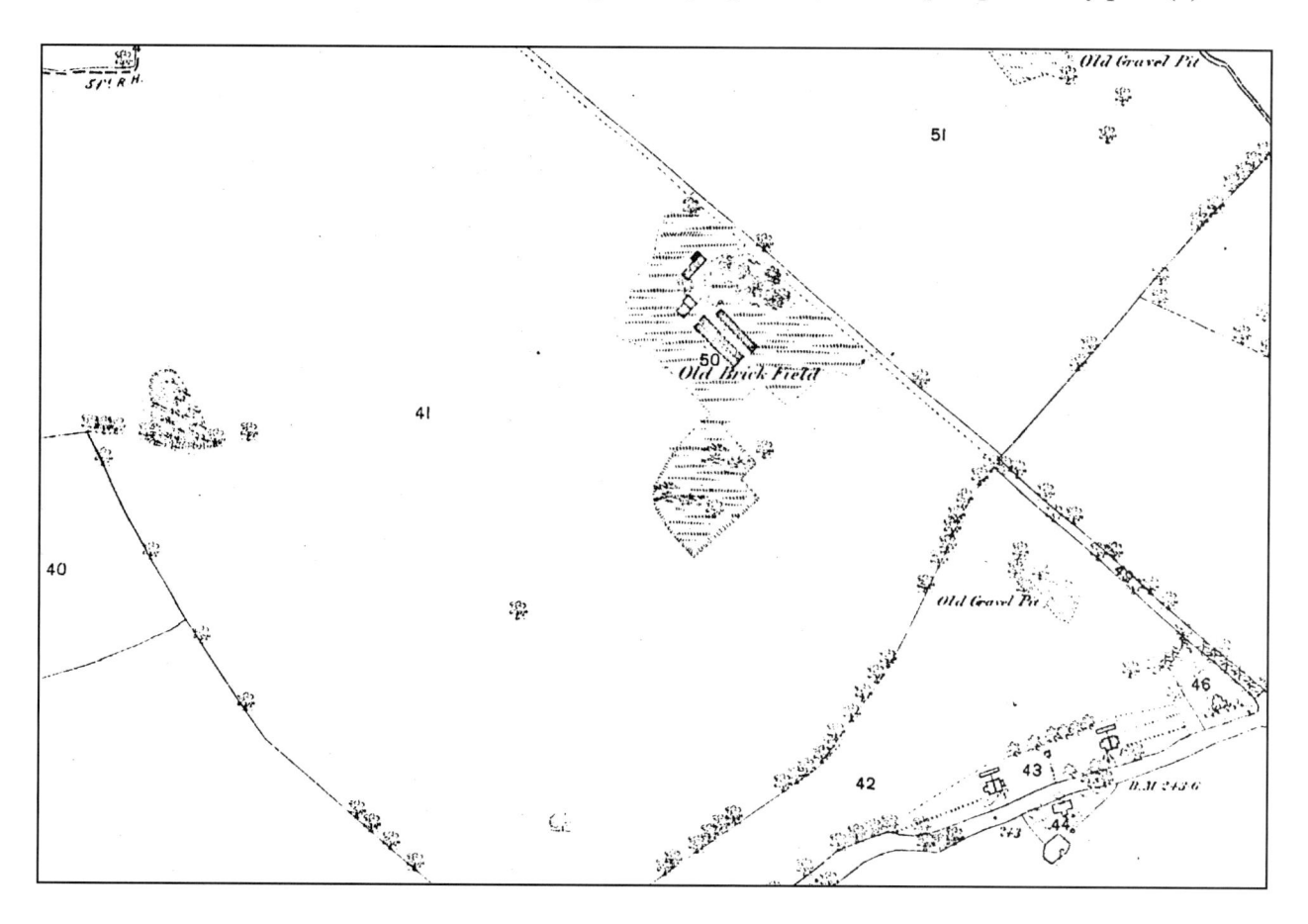

Brick Works off Park Hall Road, Gosfield from the 1876 Ordnance Survey map of 25 inches to one mile scale.

Among the employees was Harry Willett (1869-1950) who was a brother in law of George Corder. Unfortunately the Gosfield Brick Works was not successful and was closed and sold in 1895. George Corder then became a brickburner for Mark Gentry at the Langthorne Brick Works, Wethersfield Road, Sible Hedingham and Harry Willett became a tilemaker for William Corder and later for Harry Corder (1873-1942) at the Southey Green Brick, Tile and Pottery Works at Sible Hedingham.

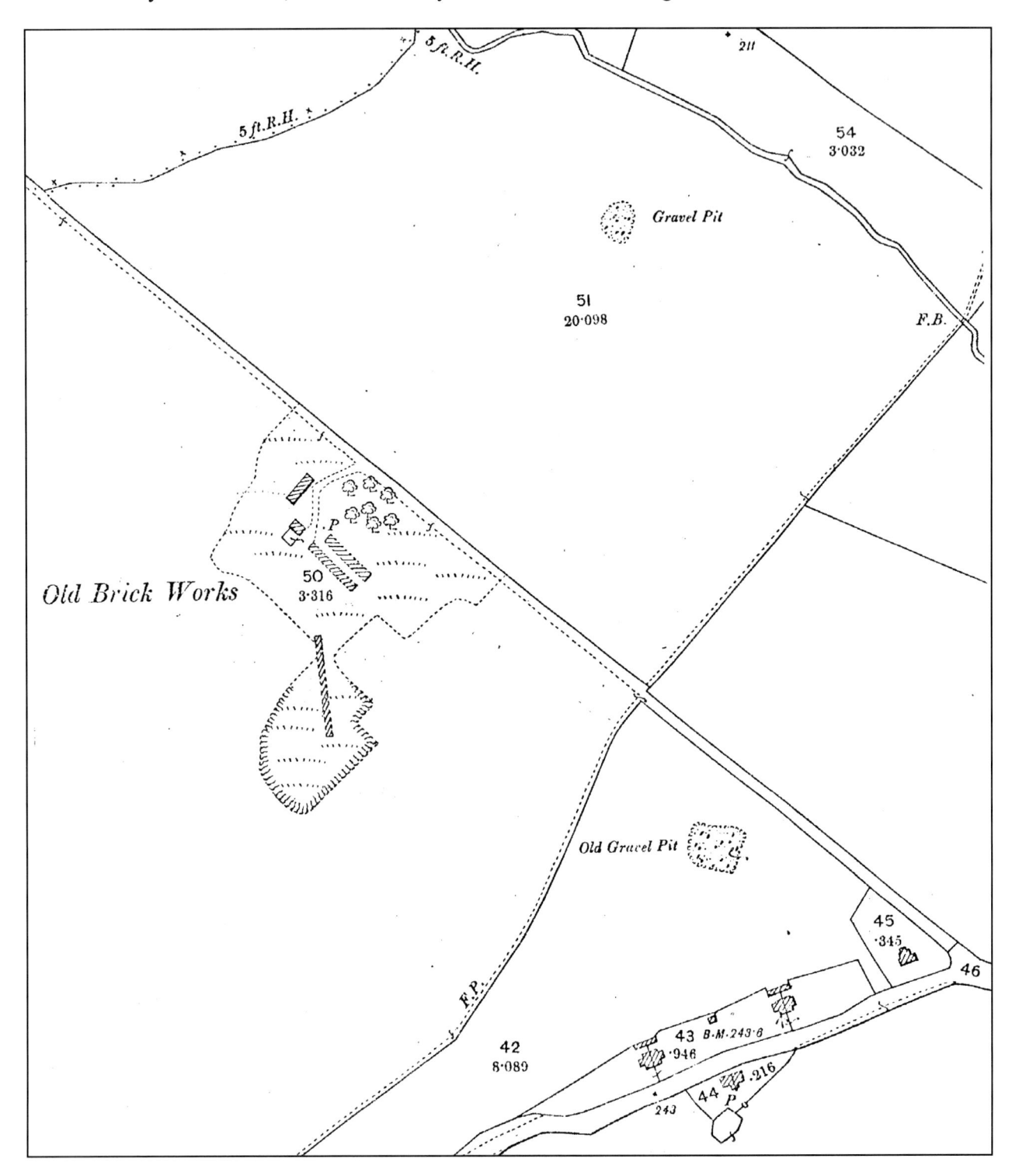

The 1897 Ordnance Survey Map showing the Brick Works surveyed shortly after closure in 1895.

The two areas of woodland in the above photographs, taken by the author in 1985, are the site of the former brickworks off Park Hall Road, Gosfield.

The Park Hall Road Brick Works was on part of the Gosfield Hall Estate and was an example of an estate brickworks. It operated intermittently depending upon demand and during the nineteenth century its status changed from an estate brickworks to being leased to a master brickmaker. Its closure in 1895 brought an end to earthenware manufacture in Gosfield after a period of some six hundred years. Pottery was made in the thirteenth and fourteenth centuries followed by bricks from the first half of the sixteenth century. The building of Gosfield Hall commenced about 1545 with red bricks made on the estate. Later additions and reconstructions, at different periods, were also in red brick when improvements to the Church were carried out by the Hall's owners in similar brickwork. The Gosfield Hall Estate Brick Works was producing bricks in 1782 when Earl Nugent supplied 41,000 bricks to Isaac Slythe, a bricklayer and mason of Colchester, towards the erection of the House of Correction at Halstead. (2) When the Gosfield Hall Estate was advertised for sale in 1854 the particulars included reference to the estate containing *"Good Brick Earth"*. The estate extended to over two thousand acres and included many cottages and farm buildings built with red bricks made at the brickworks.

George Corder (1863-1938), brickmaker and brickburner, eldest son of William Corder for whom he managed the Gosfield Brick Works from 1890 to 1895.

Chapter 9

GEORGE CORDER (1863-1938) AND HIS SONS WILLIAM DAN CORDER (1886-1970), HERBERT CHARLES CORDER (1888-1970) AND WALTER EDWARD CORDER (1896-1983)

George Corder (1863-1938)

George Corder was born 12th February 1863 at Southey Green Brickyard, Sible Hedingham and baptised 22nd March 1863 at Castle Hedingham Chapel. He was son of William Corder (1835-1903) by his first wife Hannah Corder formerly Hannah Redgewell (1831-1867).

Although George spent the majority of his young life at Southey Green, following the death of his mother, he also lived for some time with his maternal grandparents, George and Sarah Redgewell, at the Eleven Elms Public House, Crouch Green, Castle Hedingham.

George was initially a harness maker, circa 1881, (1) but by 1885 he was a brickmaker and continued in the trade, mainly as a brick burner, for the remainder of his working life. At the time of his marriage to Alice Ann Willett (1861-1927) on 6th April 1885 at Sible Hedingham Church, he was 22 years old and a brickmaker employed by his father at Southey Green.

In about 1890 George and Alice Corder, with their two eldest sons, moved from Queen Street, Sible Hedingham to Park Hall Road, Gosfield where George managed the Gosfield Brick Works for his father. In 1891 (2) the family were recorded living in Gosfield Road (now Park Hall Road) Gosfield when George's occupation was recorded as a *'Brick Maker'*.

Upon the closure of the Gosfield Brick Works in 1895, George became a brickmaker journeyman and brick burner for Mark Gentry (1850-1912) at the Langthorne Brick Works, Wethersfield Road, Sible Hedingham. George, Alice and family moved into one of the twelve cottages called *'Brickyard Cottages'* built by Mark Gentry for his employees in 1886 and 1887 in Wethersfield Road, which was then usually recorded as Oldens Road. (3) (Interestingly, Edward John Corder (1886-1938) and Henrietta Jane Corder (1883-1973) and their family later lived in another one of these Brickyard Cottages). The Langthorne Brick Works was one of the largest of its kind in the Eastern Counties manufacturing hand made, hand pressed and machine made red bricks including over 600 different shaped and ornamental bricks. In the year 1903-04 Mark Gentry had the distinction of being Chairman of the Institute of Clayworkers. (4) George continued as a brick burner for Mark Gentry until the Langthorne Brick Works closed in 1911.

He then obtained employment with the Rayner family at Maiden Ley Brick Works, Castle Hedingham. George, Alice and family then vacated their tied cottage in Wethersfield Road and moved to 4 Ethel Cottages (which later became No. 31), Alexandra Road, Sible Hedingham. George worked for the Rayner family as a brick burner from 1911 until he retired from full time employment in 1933 at the age of 70.

Alice Ann Corder nee Willett (1861-1927) in front of her home, Brickyard Cottages, Wethersfield Road, Sible Hedingham during the Edwardian era. Note the moulded brickwork to form ornamental detail either side of the first floor windows and the sunflower in the key-brick or voussoir of the gauged brickwork of the Georgian or flat arch over each door and window. This is one of two terraces of red brick cottages built by Mark Gentry for his employees, which included George Corder.

After retiring George Corder continued to take an active interest in the brickworks and visited it frequently. From 1933 until towards the end of 1937 he was often called upon to make special bricks until he completely retired through ill health, at the age of 74 years, just a few months before his death on 23rd April 1938 aged 75 years. It was George Corder who taught the owner, George Rayner, how to fire the kilns.

George and Alice had six children of whom two sons were employed in the brickmaking industry and another son made brick moulds for a short time.

The kilns at the Langthorne Brick Works, Wethersfield Road, Sible Hedingham with stacks of newly fired bricks in the foreground. On the left are the hacks for drying the 'green' bricks. George Corder was a burner and fired these kilns from 1895 until 1911. (Photograph from the Brickbuilder, April 1898 - reproduced courtesy of The British Library Board).

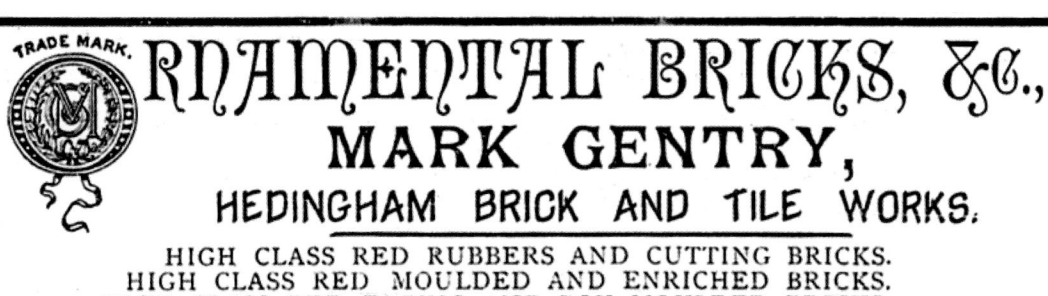

ORNAMENTAL BRICKS, &c.,
MARK GENTRY,
HEDINGHAM BRICK AND TILE WORKS.

HIGH CLASS RED RUBBERS AND CUTTING BRICKS.
HIGH CLASS RED MOULDED AND ENRICHED BRICKS.
HIGH CLASS RED FACING AND BOX MOULDED BRICKS.
ARCHITECTS SHOULD CALL AND INSPECT THE SAMPLES AT SHOW ROOMS.
CATALOGUES NOW IN HAND WITH SUGGESTIONS.
PARTS 1 & 2 WILL BE SENT POST FREE ON APPLICATION.

| WORKS, HEDINGHAM, ESSEX. | POSTAL & TELEGRAPHIC ADDRESS, SIBLE HEDINGHAM, ESSEX. | WORKS, HEDINGHAM, ESSEX. |

William Dan Corder (1886-1970)

William Dan Corder was born 27th November 1886 at Queen Street, Sible Hedingham, the eldest son of George Corder (1863-1938). Upon leaving school William was apprenticed to Harry Walter William Gooch who carried on a successful joiners, builders, contractors and grist milling business in Sible Hedingham. Harry Gooch lived in a red brick and tiled house, which he built in Swan Street and named 'Zeerust' (now 150 Swan Street) in memory of his son who lost his life in the Boer War. He had his workshops, timber sheds, paint and lime stores at the rear. The apprenticeship indenture provided that William learnt the trade of carpenter and joiner from 16th June 1902 for four years. His wages were 2/6d per week for the first year, 3/6d per week for the second year, 4/6d per week for the third year and 5/6d per week for the fourth year. The indenture was dated 1st September 1902 and signed by Harry Gooch and George Corder. Their signatures were witnessed by Robert L. Webb, who was employed in the office of Mark Gentry, the Master Brickmaker. At the end of the four year term Harry Gooch endorsed the following on the reverse of the indenture:

> *"William Dan Corder has been a quiet, steady, willing, honest and obliging young man, during his apprenticeship with me, and at his trade a good workman. (signed) Harry Gooch. June 16th 1906."* (5)

Whilst employed by Harry Gooch, William Corder's work included making wooden brick moulds, particularly for Mark Gentry. Many of these moulds were for ornamental bricks and were carved out of very hard wood, such as from well seasoned beech or pear and apple. Some of these moulds are still in use at Bulmer Brick and Tile Works over one hundred years later. Harry Gooch sold his property and business in 1909 following which moulds were made by Charles Robert Ling, who was a printer, builder, carpenter and undertaker in Castle Hedingham. Thereafter the brick moulds were made by Bert William Corder (1889-1955) (see chapter 11).

In 1909 William became a carpenter and joiner at Rippers Joinery works, and with the exception of his First World War Service in the Essex Regiment and later in the Royal Engineers, he remained with Rippers Limited until he retired in about April 1959 at over 72 years of age. He died on 15th November 1970 aged 83 years.

In August 1914 William was one of the first men in Sible Hedingham to volunteer for service and following training he was sent to France. In 1918 he was hit in the side by a bullet, which was later removed and he was fortunate to have survived. He was engaged to Bessie Turner (1888-1918) and upon his return to Sible Hedingham in late November 1918 he learnt the sad news that Bessie had died a few days earlier in the bad 'flu epidemic. (6) Bessie was the only daughter of John and Ellen Turner of Colne Engaine and later of Earls Colne. John was a native of Gestingthorpe where in 1881 (7) he was recorded as a *'Brickyard Labourer'* at the age of 13 years. He married Ellen Smith in 1887 and moved to Colne Engaine where he was employed as a brickmaker and later as a tilemaker by Pudney and Son for 31 years.

Willian Dan Corder a carpenter whose work included making wooden brick moulds including carving moulds for ornamental bricks.

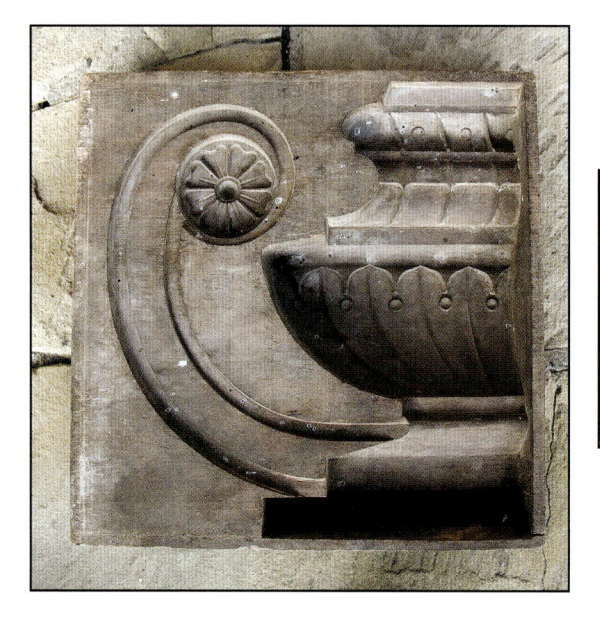

A selection of wooden brick moulds used in Sible Hedingham. These moulds were similar to those made by William Dan Corder and Bert William Corder.

Herbert Charles Corder (1888-1970)

Herbert Charles Corder was always known as Charles Corder. He was the second son of George Corder (1863-1938).

Upon leaving school Charles worked for a few years for Oliver Wallace at Brook Farm, Sible Hedingham, prior to Rippers factory and houses being built on the land. In circa 1911 he was employed as a bricklayer's labourer followed by employment at Crittalls Works in Braintree circa 1914.

During the First World War he served in the Army Service Corps and following his discharge he worked for the Rayner family at Maiden Ley Brick Works, Castle Hedingham, until the outbreak of the Second World War: a period of twenty years.

Although the Rayner family employed many men in their brickworks, Charles Corder was their only full time employee. In view of the seasonal nature of brickmaking, the other men worked a fortnight on and a fortnight off during the winter months, whilst digging out clay for the following year.

Charles was responsible for firing the kilns, working mainly at night whilst his father fired the kilns during the day. Apart from George and Charles Corder no other employees were qualified to burn the bricks and the Rayner family always held them in high regard. Throughout much of this time there were six kilns working although latterly, during the ownership of George Rayner only four of these kilns were used. The largest kiln held 33,000 bricks and the smallest 21,000 bricks. There was usually only one or two kilns burning at any one time because of the approximate ten day cycle taken to load, fire, cool and empty each kiln.

On 7th June 1931 shortly before 1.30am there was an earthquake in north Essex which was felt by the Rayner family in their nearby farm house. However Charles Corder, who was on top of a kiln during the course of firing it, was not aware of the severe tremor. It was the biggest and broadest earth tremor recorded in England since the Colchester earthquake of 1884. Fortunately no loss of life or any really serious damage resulted. (8)

Charles was also the engine driver at Maiden Ley Brick Works and operated the engines which turned the pug mills. Upon the outbreak of war on 3rd September 1939 the brickworks closed for the duration because of the blackout regulations and the risk of pilots of hostile aircraft seeing the fires from these updraught kilns, which would have made a good navigation beacon. On the day war was declared a kiln was being fired and the bricks had commenced burning. The Police arrived and ordered the fires to be put out until after the war. In 1945 the burning of these bricks resumed and most of them were found to be satisfactory. In 1939 Charles found employment as an engine driver with Samuel Courtauld Limited at their Bocking Mill until his retirement in 1954. He died on 20th November 1970 aged 81 years.

Herbert Charles Corder who was a brick burner for the Rayner family at Maiden Ley Brick Works, Castle Hedingham, between the two wars. This photograph was taken during the First World War when he served in the Army Service Corps.

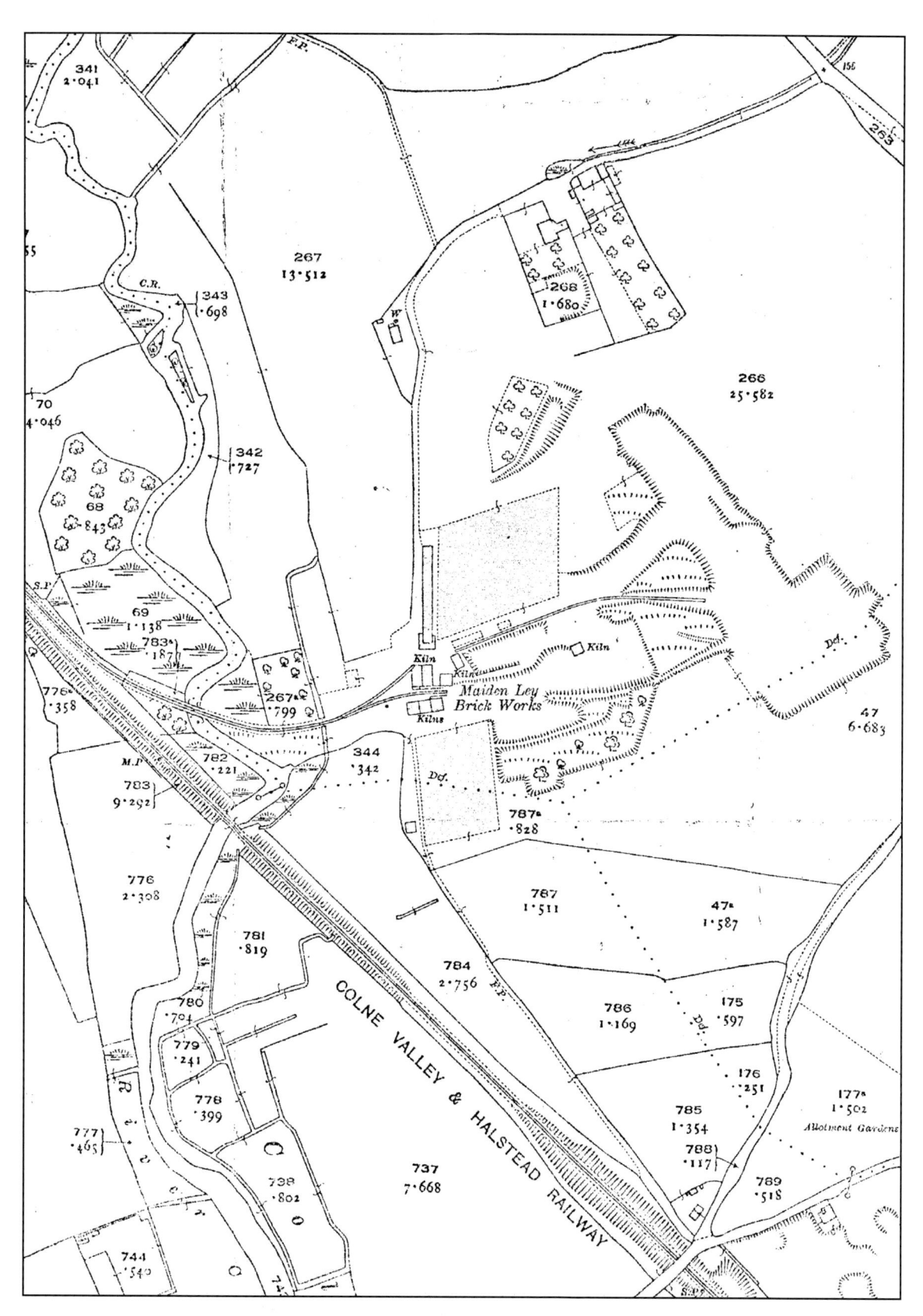

Maiden Ley Brick Works from the Ordnance Survey Map 1922 showing the siding from the Colne Valley and Halstead Railway and the tramway from the clay pits to the brickmaking area. The map shows five kilns, which were fired by George Corder from 1911 until 1933 and by his son Charles from 1919 until 1939.

Maiden Ley Brick Works from the rear of Swan Street, Sible Hedingham, overlooking the River Colne. Note the waggon on the railway siding in the centre, a kiln on the right and the long drying shed on the left.

Another view of Maiden Ley Brick Works photographed the same day from the opposite direction, with the kiln in the centre, hacks on the left and drying and brick making sheds on the right.

Walter Edward Corder (1896-1983)

Walter Edward Corder was born 3rd February 1896 at Brickyard Cottages, Wethersfield Road, Sible Hedingham, the youngest of four sons of George Corder (1863-1938).

Upon leaving the National School at Sible Hedingham he became an agricultural worker for Walter Whitlock, a farmer and chaff merchant at Poole Farm, Great Yeldham. On 22nd November 1915 he enlisted as a rifleman in the King's Royal Rifle Corps, in which his uncle John Corder and cousin Percy Corder also served. Walter saw action in France and was disabled when a shell burst close to him causing concussion and knocking him out. He eventually recovered sufficiently and became fit enough to be transferred into the Labour Corps to continue useful service as a guard at the Okehampton POW camp in Devon. (9).

Following the end of the First World War he was given the choice of working for his uncle, Harry Corder, at the Southey Green Brick, Tile and Pottery Works or working for his father's first cousin, Frank Redgewell Twitchett, on his farms at Clare and Belchamp St. Paul. (10). He chose working as a tilemaker for Harry Corder and therefore became the fourth generation of the Corder family to make clay products at Southey Green. He was principally a tilemaker but in the early 1920's he occasionally helped his uncle, Fred Corder, with delivering bricks, tiles and other products by horses and cart.

Walter worked at Southey Green until the outbreak of the Second World War, apart from a short break of one season (one year) at Bulmer Brick Works, during the 1930's. On 18th November 1939 he represented the Corder family at the funeral of Eli Cornish, CC., JP., a Sible Hedingham master brickmaker.

In September 1939 production ceased at many locations including Southey Green, owing to the risk of enemy night raiders seeing the fires from up draught kilns. Walter then worked for a short time for The Sible Hedingham Red Brick Company Limited, which was able to operate with its down draught kilns because the fires could be adequately covered during the blackout. During the Second World War he served in the Castle Hedingham Platoon of the Home Guard and interestingly some of their exercises took place at The Sible Hedingham Red Brick Company's works at Purls Hill, Sible Hedingham and at Maiden Ley Brick Works at Castle Hedingham. On one occasion a kiln at Maiden Ley was accidentally destroyed. During the war Walter left The Sible Hedingham Red Brick Company Limited and transferred to its parent company, Rippers Limited, joinery manufacturers, where he remained until he retired in 1961. Thereafter he worked part time at Hedingham Castle for Miss. Musette Majendie, C.B.E., and Dr. Margery Blackie, M.D., M.B., B.S., L.R.C.P., M.R.C.S., C.V.O., (Physician to Queen Elizabeth II from 1969 to 1979).

Walter died on 18th June 1983 aged 87 years. Walter's wife, Ethel Mary Corder nee Sams (1896-1983), who had also worked at Hedingham Castle, died three days later on 21st June and a double funeral was held at Sible Hedingham Church on 24th June 1983.

Walter Edward Corder in 1928

Walter Edward Corder left and William Jonathan Heels (1906-1982) right in July 1980 standing at the end of the former pipe making shed, garage and barn at Southey Green, which was converted into stables. William Heels was the son of Mary Heels nee Corder (1860-1923). Walter and William were first cousins and two of the grandsons of William Corder (1835-1903).

Chapter 10

BRICK KILN HILL BRICK WORKS, CASTLE HEDINGHAM, ROBERT CORDER (1833-1915) AND FAMILY

Robert Corder (1833-1915)

Robert Corder was the eldest son of John Corder (1806-1880) and Susan Corder nee Ives (1809-1877). He was born at Gestingthorpe and when old enough he followed his father into the brickmaking industry, initially at Gestingthorpe and later, from circa 1848, at Castle Hedingham.

Robert is recorded on all census returns from 1851 to 1901 inclusive as a *'brick maker'*. In circa 1881 he lived at Southey Green, Sible Hedingham, when he was employed by his younger brother, William Corder (1835-1903) as a brickmaker. However, Robert was employed for the majority of his working life by successive owners of the brickworks at Brick Kiln Hill, Castle Hedingham. He specialised in making pamments and was manager of these brickworks for many years when owned by Thomas Moy Limited.

Under the management of Robert Corder the following products were supplied:
"*Plain, Gutter, Roof, Pan and other Tiles, Floor and Stable Bricks, Splays, Squints, Red Facings, etc.*"

In 1896 a new kiln was constructed for which details survive. The builders were George Hardy & Son of Great Yeldham, from whom William Corder had purchased the Potter's Hall Brick Yard at Great Yeldham in 1892. The construction commenced on 28th February and was completed on 6th May 1896. The brick built kiln was constructed on a concrete base. The number of bricklayers and labourers engaged each day and the daily cost is recorded. The maximum cost for 2 bricklayers and 4 labourers was 18/- a day. During a two month period 17 bags of lime at 2/- each was supplied. The total cost of construction including bricklayers, labourers and supply of lime was £34 0s 0d.

The kiln was 13 foot 10 inches square (outside work). The total number of bricks used, which were clearly made on site, was 65,646 and it took 632 bricks to one course all round square work. The break down was as follows:

Bottom of kiln to the top of the floor including arches	*8750 bricks*
"Corners and thick work" (buttresses)	*5000 bricks*
Square work to kiln	*49296 bricks*
Dome	*2000 bricks*
Chimneys	*600 bricks*
Total	*65646 bricks*

Although the records do not specify the type of kiln it was probably a square down-draught kiln because of the references to the dome and chimneys. It is interesting to note that a bricklayer and three labourers worked on Good Friday but on Easter Saturday *"all at home"* and Easter Monday was a holiday. A couple of weeks later there was *"rain all day"* and no work done. Throughout the two months a total of four days were lost through rain. Two more days were lost waiting for irons (the metalwork required for the kiln - presumably kiln bars, grates and furnace doors). Two of the workmen were named as Harry and Eli Gurteen and the work they carried out for one day cost 4/-. Apart from the construction records, (1) the kiln itself does not survive and was removed following closure of the brickworks.

Robert Corder (1833-1915)

In May 1897 Robert suffered an accident whilst engaged in carrying out a new plan of loading the kiln for burning, the process being calculated to produce a better surface. While on top of the kiln in the act of unloading, a portion of the bricks fell upon him and forced him off the kiln, thus causing a fall of some feet and the bricks fell upon him causing considerable injury to his foot. He was wheeled home in a wheelbarrow to his cottage overlooking Crouch Green, Castle Hedingham. (2) Upon recovery Robert continued his work as brickmaker and manager until his retirement upon the closure of the Brick Works during the early 1900s. (3) They had closed by 1910 when the Land Value Duty Survey described the two acre site as *"land - late Brick Field"* owned and occupied by Robert Balls. (3) Robert Corder died on 2nd November 1915 aged 82 years. (4)

The site of the former brickworks at Brick Kiln Hill, Castle Hedingham in 1985

Charles Corder (1859-1938)

Charles Corder was born on 19th April 1859 at Castle Hedingham, the eldest son of Robert Corder (1833-1915) and Harriet Corder nee Parr (1834-1899).

As soon as he was old enough Charles followed his father into the brickmaking industry. On the 1871 census, (5) when Charles was 11 years old, his occupation was recorded as *"Helps Brick-Maker"*. He continued to be employed at the Brick Kiln Hill Brickworks for some years but by 1881 was living and working in London. After various occupations he was eventually employed by the Great Northern Railway and retired in 1923. He then returned to live at Pottery Lane, Castle Hedingham with his wife, Mary Hannah Corder. Charles died on 22nd March 1938 aged 78 years.

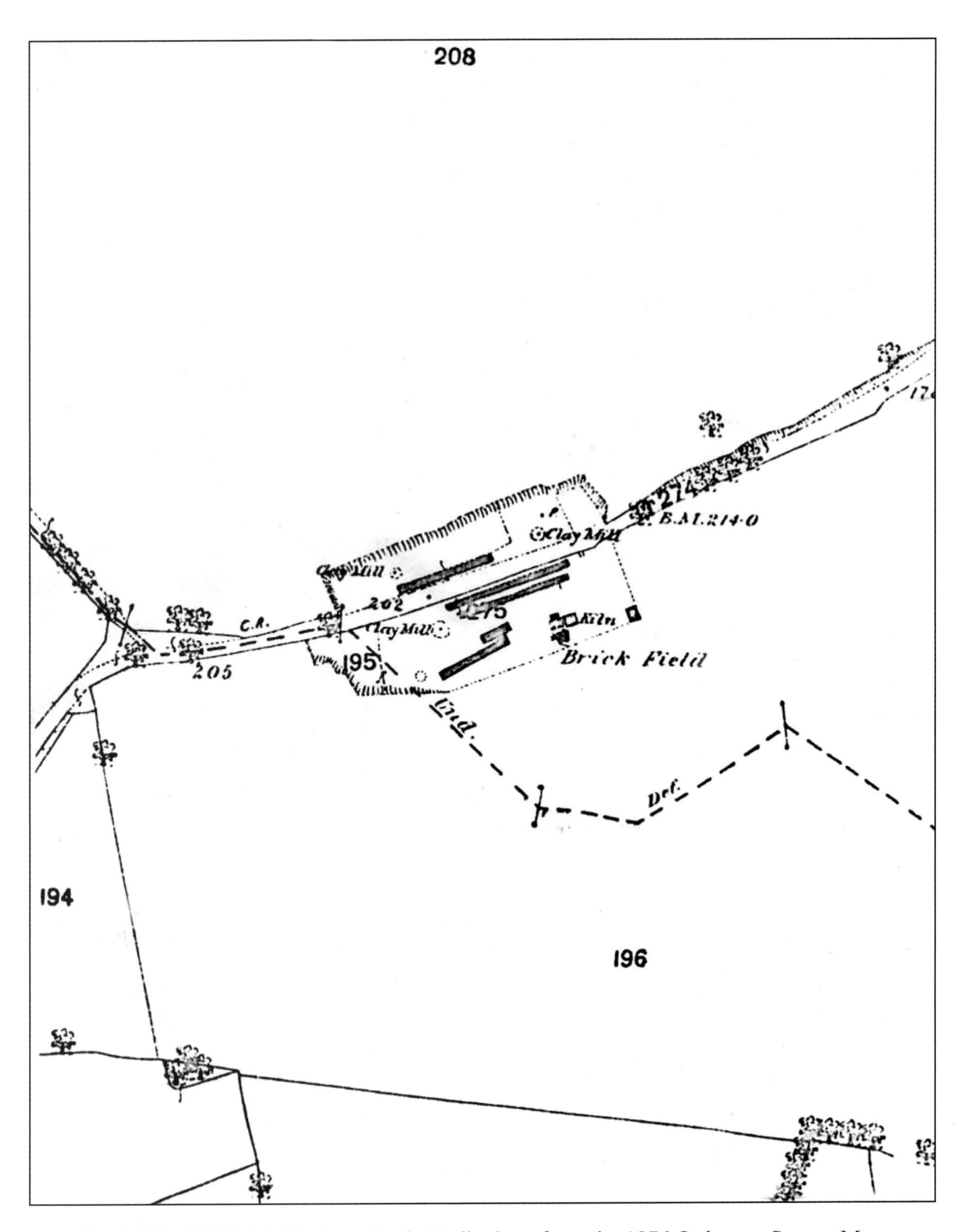

Brick Kiln Hill Brick Works at Castle Hedingham from the 1876 Ordnance Survey Map of 25 inches to one mile scale. This map shows three clay or wash mills, one kiln and rows of hacks.

Alice Edith Corder later Drury (1871-1967)

Alice Edith Corder was born 7th January 1871 at Crouch Green, Castle Hedingham and was the seventh of the eight children of Robert and Harriet Corder. On 10th February 1893 she married William Thomas Drury (1874-1939). William known as 'Buller' Drury worked successively as a farm worker, a porter for the Colne Valley and Halstead Railway and latterly for many years for Rippers Joinery works. One of his brothers, Fred Drury and two of their sisters namely Sarah Drury, later Steggles and Mary Drury known as 'Polly', worked for Edward Bingham (1829-1916) in his pottery at Castle Hedingham.

The Corder and Bingham families were related through the Parr family of Castle Hedingham. On 29th December 1853, Edward Bingham married Eliza Mary Parr Ruffle (1830-1901). Her maternal grandfather, Joseph Parr (1774-1849) was Steward to the Majendie family at Hedingham Castle for many years. Joseph Parr provided Edward Bingham with information about the history of Castle Hedingham some of which he used in a lecture delivered in December 1894, which was later published as *"Castle Hedingham in Olden Times"*. Joseph Parr's daughter, Eliza Mary Parr (1806-1883) married William Cousins Ruffle (1803-1878). On 18th May 1855 Robert Corder married Harriet Parr, a daughter of George Parr (1804-1855). One of his sisters, another Harriet Parr (1816-1890) married William Downs (1813-1904) on 24th May 1836. Their daughter, Eliza Downs (1842-1920) became the second wife of William Corder (1835-1903) in 1870.

In her later years Alice Drury provided historical information to authors for local history books. In particular she helped R. J. Bradley with his book *'Castle Hedingham Pottery (1837-1905)'*, which detailed the history of the Bingham Pottery. (6) She also shared her knowledge with Jack Lindsay for his book, *'The Discovery of Britain'*. (7) In the chapter about Edward Bingham, the following is included:

"Mrs. Drury - always called Little Mrs. Drury - knew Richard (Bingham) well; Edward Corder was her brother. She is 85 years old; but you could knock twenty years or more off and still say she looked young for her age. ....She lived beside the Bingham house in the old days; and her mother used to help Mrs. Edward Bingham with her regular progeny. When her brother went off with Dick (Richard Bingham), he promised his parents to come back in six years and he did having had many knocks in the meantime. .... Her own family had much to do with brickyards. Her father was foreman at the brickworks up the hill from Crouch Green; as a child she lost part of a finger when she and a brother played about with the machinery, "I didn't mind much, but we both yelled out so loud they didn't know which was hurt" Her father made the hard lightish floor-bricks. Her brother Edward, who went off with Dick Bingham, after two voyages, came home then worked elsewhere at brickworks that were closed in the 1914 war; after serving in the army he tried another brickworks, then a shop. ....The Corder with the brickworks at Southey Green was an uncle. ....There used to be a patch of white clay, Mrs. Drury said, near the pile-bridge, the local name for the railway bridge over the stream below Crouch Green. ...."

On the subject of fights, brawls, invaders and gangs from Halstead, particularly at elections when gangs broke up meetings:

"Mrs. Drury says that they had a whistle which they blew when things were going to be violent. She heard the whistle this time and at once began closing doors and windows, and barricading them. She adds that the brick-makers had been wanting to teach the invaders a lesson for some time."

More information about these incidents would be interesting but is now lost. Alice Drury died on 6th January 1967 on the day before her 96th birthday and at the time of her death was the oldest person in Castle Hedingham.

The Bingham family and employees at The Pottery, Castle Hedingham circa 1900. Left to right: unknown, unknown, Frederick Drury, Edward Bingham (1829-1916), unknown, Edward William Bingham (1863-1919), Martha Dyson (later Boorer), Mrs. Hephzibah Bingham (wife of Edward William), Agnes Dyson (later Hilsden), Mary (Polly) Drury, unknown, unknown and Annie Kendall (later Wright). The unknown persons are believed to be members of the Bingham family. Note the hats hanging on the brick wall, which still stands in the garden of Pottery Cottage.

Edward Bingham (1829-1916) at work in his pottery.

These two similar items show the difference between glazed and earthenware pottery made at Castle Hedingham and Sible Hedingham Potteries respectively. The green glazed ware on the left was made by Edward Bingham at Castle Hedingham and includes a lid, the handle of which is an ornamental dog. The red earthenware piece on the right was made by Harry Corder at Southey Green Brick, Tile and Pottery Works. It is a flower pot, which has had many years use causing the white staining around the lower half.

Benjamin Smith (1879-1939)

Benjamin Smith was born at Great Yeldham, the youngest son of Philip and Sarah Smith who moved to Nunnery Street, Castle Hedingham circa 1888. One of Benjamin's elder brothers was Harry Smith who circa 1891 was a labourer in the Ornamental Pottery owned by Edward Bingham (1829-1916) at Castle Hedingham.

In 1901 Benjamin married Ellen Corder (1873-1912), known as Nellie, who was the youngest of the eight children of Robert and Harriet Corder. Benjamin was employed as a brickmaker at the Brick Kiln Hill Brick Works, Castle Hedingham, where his father in law Robert Corder was manager. In fact at the time of the 1901 census, Benjamin and Nellie Smith were living in the household of her father, Robert Corder at Crouch Green, Castle Hedingham.

Whilst working as a brickmaker, Benjamin Smith made a man's head in terracotta. It was described by Jack Lindsay in his book, *'The Discovery of Britain'* (8) as:

"an odd battered face with eagle-nose in red terracotta"

When Leonard Smith (Benjamin's son) moved from Crouch Green to Trinity Cottage, Castle Hedingham, the terracotta head accompanied him and was located in his front garden. It remained at Trinity Cottage until Leonard Smith's death in 1983.

The Smith family outside their cottage at Crouch Green, Castle Hedingham about 1911. Left to right: Ellen Smith nee Corder (1873-1912) holding Lily Maud (1910-1999), Benjamin is holding Leonard Ernest (1907-1983). To the left of the door is the head of the man in terracotta made by Benjamin.

By 1911 Benjamin was employed by T. Bradridge & Co, coal and corn merchants of The Maltings, Station Road, Sible Hedingham as a 'coal carman' (coal delivery man) using a horse and tumbril. He later worked as a coalman for Thomas Moy Limited, coal merchants, from their depot in Station Road, when he continued to deliver coal from a horse drawn cart. He died on 18th August 1939 following an accident.

Benjamin Smith when a coalman for Thomas Moy Limited by whom he was previously employed as a brickmaker. The name 'MOY' can be seen on the horse brass and on the cart. This photograph was taken circa 1930 opposite his home at Crouch Green, Castle Hedingham.

Chapter 11

JOHN CORDER (1863-1957) AND HIS THREE SONS EDWARD JOHN CORDER (1886-1938), BERT WILLIAM CORDER (1889-1955) AND PERCY JAMES CORDER (1896-1989)

John Corder (1863-1957)

John Corder was born 4th June 1863 at Crouch Green, Castle Hedingham, the second son of Robert Corder (1833-1915) and Harriet Corder nee Parr (1834-1899)

John Corder (1863-1957)

John started farm work at seven years of age for Francis Whitlock of Lovingtons Farm and for his son Walter Whitlock of Poole Farm, Great Yeldham. His initial duties included singling mangold, scaring birds, stone picking and other agricultural work. He remained a farm worker for some ten years but inevitably followed family tradition and went into the brickmaking industry. He was initially a labourer at Brick Kiln Hill Brick Works, Castle Hedingham, which was managed by his father. John married Alice Agnes Brett on 9th May 1884 and their four children were born between 1886 and 1896 at Nunnery Street, Castle Hedingham, where the family lived.

By 1901 (1) the family had moved to New England, Sible Hedingham, when John was employed as a brick burner by Mark Gentry of the Hedingham Brick and Tile Works at his Highfield Brick Works. In 1911, John and his eldest son Edward were both employed as brick and tile makers at The Manor Brickworks, Thundersley, which was managed by John's younger brother Edward. (2) At around the time of the First World War John was employed for a comparatively short time by Thomas Moy Limited as a coal carter/coalman in the Hedinghams and Yeldhams and as a brickmaker by his cousin, Harry Corder (1873-1942) at the Southey Green Brick, Tile and Pottery Works.

The Hedingham Brick and Tile Works at Highfield, owned by Mark Gentry. John Corder is on top of the kiln and his eldest son, Edward John Corder (1886-1938) is standing on the extreme left. The man in the foreground with bowler hat is the manager, Daniel Cornish. This view, which is featured on the front cover of this book shows newly fired bricks being unloaded from a kiln, using crowding barrows and loaded into the trucks on a siding from the Colne Valley and Halstead Railway.

The Hedingham Brick and Tile Works with up-draught kilns and part of the railway siding in the right foreground. John Corder who was brick burner here for upwards of 50 years is second from the right. In the left background is a chimney in the course of erection with scaffolding around. This chimney is for the downdraught kilns. The bricks on the extreme left are ordinary bricks but those in front of the chimney appear to be bullnose/ squints. This photograph was probably taken circa 1905 by William Wright Raynham when he was the foreman.

During the first two decades of the 1900s John was also employed by the Hedingham Brick Company at the Purls Hill Brick Works, when it was owned by Eli Cornish. In 1919 The Sible Hedingham Red Brick Company Limited was incorporated to take over the former brickworks of Mark Gentry at Highfield and Eli Cornish at Purls Hill, which were adjacent to each other. The initial directors were Tucker Ripper, Charlton Ripper, Eli Cornish and Reuben Hunt. (3) John Corder fired the kilns continuously for The Sible Hedingham Red Brick Company Limited from 1919 until his retirement in 1938 at the age of 75 years when he was succeeded by Albert Redgewell.

John initially fired six up draught kilns and latterly three down draught kilns, which took about three or four days and nights for each kiln. During this time John stayed in a small wooden hut at the brickworks where he had a good store of home made wine hidden away, which he shared with family and friends, when they visited him at the brickworks.

He died on 2nd January 1957 at the age of 93 years.

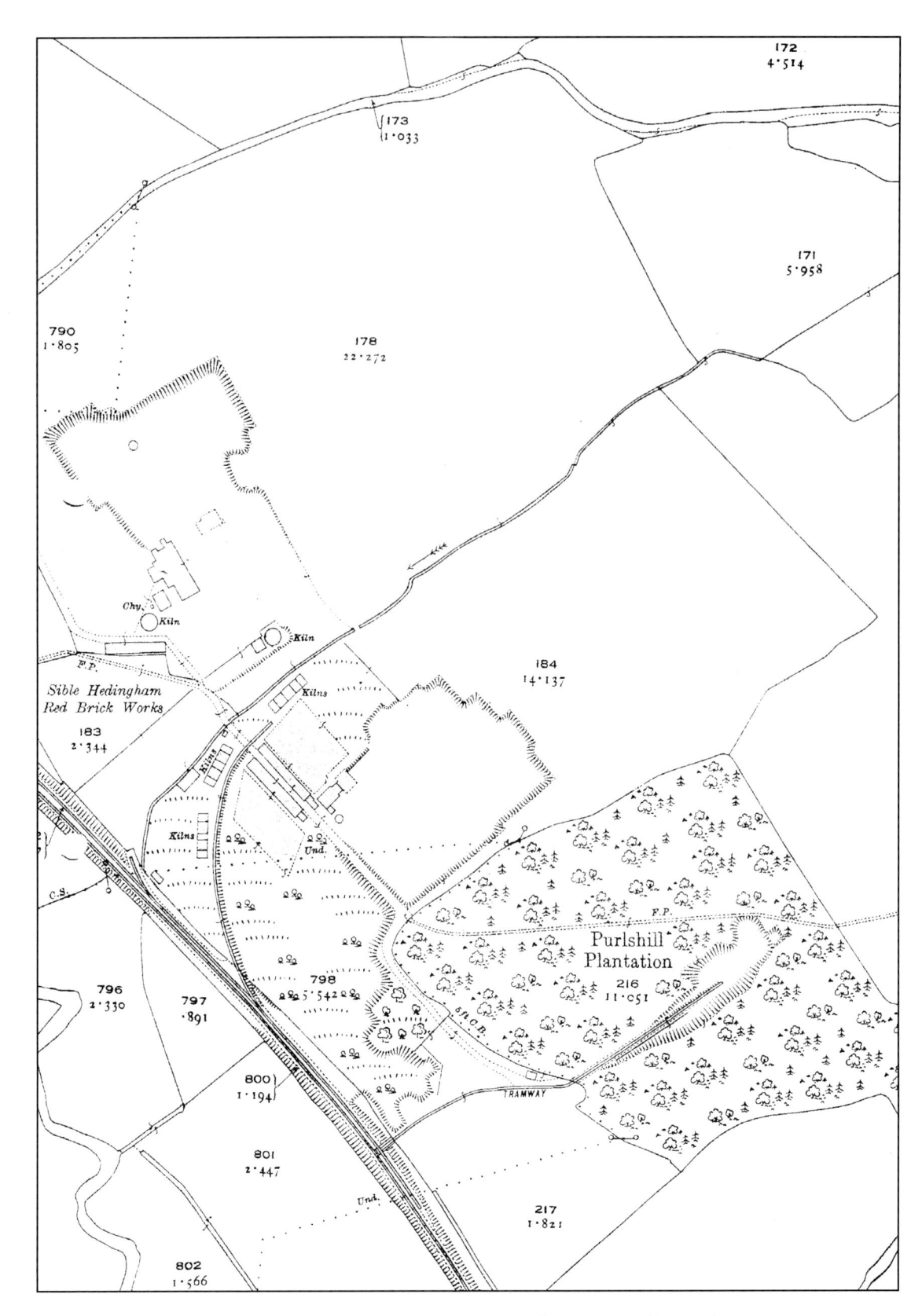

Sible Hedingham Red Brick Works from the 25 inch to one mile Ordnance Survey map of 1922, with the kilns, which were fired by John Corder. Also featured is the siding from the Colne Valley and Halstead Railway and the tramway into the sand pits in Purls Hill Plantation.

The Sible Hedingham Red Brick Company Limited showing the three down draught kilns, two chimneys with the hacks and drying sheds in the centre background. John Corder fired these kilns until his retirement in 1938 at the age of 75 years.

Edward John Corder (1886-1938)

Edward John Corder (1886-1938)

Edward John Corder was born 3rd April 1886, the eldest son of John Corder (1863-1957) and Alice Agnes Corder nee Brett (1863-1951). From an early age, Ted, as he was known and his two younger brothers, Bert and Percy helped their father, with work at the Hedingham Brick and Tile Works at Highfield, Sible Hedingham. One of their earliest jobs was to 'skintle' the 'green' bricks: that is to turn them round in the hacks so that they could dry out evenly.

In the 1901 census, (4) at the age of 14 years, Ted's employment is recorded as *'Odd Work at Brick Works - worker'*. However by 1907 he was working for Rippers joinery manufacturers until 1911 when he was employed as a brick and tile maker at The Manor Brickworks, Thundersley, which were managed by his uncle Edward. (5) By 1913 Ted returned to Rippers where he remained until his death on 6th August 1938. Following his marriage to Henrietta Jane Post (1883-1973) in 1913 they lived in Brickyard Cottages, Wethersfield Road, Sible Hedingham. They had two children, Dorothy Olive Corder later Bright (1916-1999) and Edward Stanley Corder (1918-1998). Edward worked for Rippers from 1933 to 1983 apart from his war service with REME in the Far East.

Bert William Corder (1889-1955)

Bert Corder was born 19th February 1889 at Castle Hedingham, the second son of John Corder (1863-1957).

While at school Bert carried out odd jobs, including skintling bricks under the supervision of his father, at Mark Gentry's Hedingham Brick and Tile Works. Upon leaving school he served his apprenticeship in the building trade as a carpenter with Rippers; then a comparatively small concern. In 1924 he commenced business in partnership with Charles Horace Palmer trading as Palmer and Corder, builders and contractors and later continued the business on his own account trading as B. W. Corder, as a master builder and contractor, decorator, carpenter, joiner, cabinet maker and undertaker.

Bert Corder made wooden moulds for local brickmakers, principally during the period from 1924 to 1939. These included wooden moulds for various types of roofing tiles as well as for bricks including ornamental bricks. The moulds were made of well-seasoned beech-wood or from fruit trees such as apple and pear. The moulds were large enough to allow for shrinkage of the clay during the drying and burning process. Among his customers was his father's cousin, Harry Corder of the Southey Green Brick, Tile and Pottery Works and the Rayner family at Maiden Ley Brick Works, Castle Hedingham.

Bert was a member of a number of organisations including the Sible Hedingham Rifle Club, the WEA, and the Hedinghams Brass Band of which his elder brother, Ted, was also a member. Bert was a long standing Councillor with Sible Hedingham Parish Council becoming Vice Chairman. In 1931 he was proposed for Chairman but declined to accept. He carried out considerable work over many years in connection with the maintenance of the Recreation Ground in Sible Hedingham.

Bert William Corder in his builders yard at Sible Hedingham.

As a builder he carried out a large number of building contracts for various local authorities including the former Halstead Rural District Council, Halstead Urban District Council and Belchamp Rural District Council. These were mainly for the erection and maintenance of Council Houses and Bungalows in Halstead, Sible Hedingham, Gestingthorpe, Toppesfield, Alphamstone, Belchamp St. Paul, Great and Little Yeldham. He owned two Morris lorries (PU 4266 and PU 6420), which he used to collect bricks, tiles and other building materials from local brickworks for building sites where he was working. He also owned and drove a Standard motor car.

Following Bert's sudden death on 12th January 1955 (6) the business was continued by his son, Kenneth Frederick Corder, who continued to trade as B. W. Corder, until his retirement in 1987.

Bert William Corder and Lewis Boorer with a Morris lorry, PU 4266, purchased from Frank Watson of Bocking. This was one of two lorries owned by B. W. Corder for his building construction business. His other lorry, also a Morris, PU 6420, was acquired second hand from George Goodchild, a farmer of Great Yeldham Hall. It was part of the payment for the cost of building work carried out in 1929-30 when B. W. Corder converted a former granary into two cottages at Potters Hall Farm (see page 65). This lorry was described as a pneumatic tyre tilt lorry with false bottom. It had been purchased by George Goodchild on 21st September 1928 at an auction at Potters Hall. The previous owners were Cecil and Kate Usher (7). Kate Usher was a daughter of Charles Bocking who had succeeded William Corder at the former Potters Hall Brick Works some thirty years earlier (see chapter 7).

FROM 'Phone 17	Alexandra Road 2718
B. W. CORDER	Sible Hedingham
BUILDER and CONTRACTOR	ESSEX
JOINER and CABINET MAKER	June 1st 1946

B. W. CORDER

Builder and Contractor

SIBLE HEDINGHAM

Have pleasure in announcing they are extending their business to Halstead and District.

First - class Tradesmen employed, guaranteeing a really good job at competitive prices.

Joinery manufacturing a speciality.

Estimates for large or small jobs given free, without obligation.

Phone Hedingham 185.

Telephone: HEDINGHAM 185

B. W. CORDER

BUILDER and CONTRACTOR

Joiner and Cabinet Maker

Every branch of the trade covered, including—
HOT AND COLD WATER FITTING.
CENTRAL HEATING.
DECORATING.
RECONDITIONING AND REPAIRS TO AGRICULTURAL BUILDINGS A SPECIALITY.

ESTIMATES AND PLANS PREPARED

ALEXANDRA ROAD
SIBLE HEDINGHAM
HALSTEAD, Essex

Advertisements of B. W. Corder. The metal manhole cover stating "B W CORDER BUILDER SIBLE HEDINGHAM" is still in use as a well cover adjacent to a pump in the garden of Hulls Mill House on the border of Sible Hedingham and Great Maplestead.

Workmen building one of two bungalows now 136 and 138 Swan Street, Sible Hedingham in 1925. The main contractor was Percy Parr, who was a builder living at Church Street, Castle Hedingham. Left to right: Albert Martin, Percy Ralph Bareham, Percy James Parr, Stanley Wilding and Harry Steward. Albert Martin and the two carpenters (with saws) worked for Bert Corder who subcontracted them to Percy Parr.

Percy Parr's grandfather, William Parr, was a brother to Harriet Parr who married Robert Corder and were the grandparents of Bert Corder. Percy Parr and Bert Corder were therefore second cousins. The roofing tiles for these bungalows were supplied by Harry Corder. One of these bungalows was built for Mrs. James Jay on whose behalf Percy Parr applied for planning permission to the former Halstead Rural District Council on 25th July 1925. The application, which was granted, provided for the drains to be connected to the public sewer and for water to be supplied from a well on site. The plans for this bungalow are deposited in the ERO (8). Percy Parr was born at Castle Hedingham on 3rd July 1893 and in November 1912 enlisted into the army. He was serving in the 2nd Suffolk Regiment when War was declared in August 1914. He was one of the first to leave England for France on 13th August, officially entered the War on 15th August and took part in the engagement at Mons on 23rd August. He went into action again at Le Cateau on 26th August and was posted as missing by his regiment after the engagement. It was not until 23rd October that his parents received a postcard from Gefangener-Lager, Doeberitz, Germany stating that he was a prisoner of war. After eighteen months in a prisoner of war camp he worked for three years in a coal mine for twelve hours a day, seven days a week. In January 1919 he returned to Hedingham after four and a half years in captivity. He became a staunch member of the British Legion and of Castle Hedingham Parish Council. As a Master Builder and Contractor he built a number of new dwellings in Castle and Sible Hedingham. He was also engaged on repair work to the Keep at Hedingham Castle following its damage by fire in 1918. He did not enjoy good health and died at Madeira House, London Road, Copford on 1st December 1942.

Percy James Corder (1896-1989)

Percy James Corder was born on 22nd July 1896 at Castle Hedingham and was the youngest son of John Corder (1863-1957).

At a young age Percy followed his two elder brothers and *'skintled'* bricks at the Hedingham Brick and Tile Works, whilst still attending school. Upon leaving school he was employed in the building industry as a bricklayer by Arthur Frank Gibson, a Sible Hedingham builder. Percy is recorded on the 1911 census as a *'bricklayer'* aged 14 years. (9)

In 1913 he helped to build the Ruffle family home at School Hill, Sible Hedingham, shown in the above photograph, using *'Hedingham reds'*. The men are left to right back row: Ben Howe and Alf Steward and front row: Tom Ward, Herb Brett, Percy Corder, Fred Ruffle and Jack Harrod.

During the First World War he served in the 9th Rifle Brigade, Kings Royal Rifle Corps, when he was seriously injured and carried the scars for the rest of his life until his death in 1989 at the age of 92 years. Percy was the last surviving former First World War serviceman in Sible Hedingham out of the 320 men who served. (10) After the War he returned to the building industry and was employed by his brother, Bert Corder, for many years. Percy also carried out some work on his own account, such as building Foxborough Hills House and was employed latterly by his nephew Kenneth who traded as B. W. Corder. In February 1951 Percy was granted a *'private building licence'* to build a bungalow on land in Alexandra Road, which he had owned since 1924. The bungalow, which was named *'Runcorn'* (now 16 Alexandra Road) became his home.

Percy James Corder (1896-1989)

Chapter 12

EDWARD CORDER (1868-1940) AND THE MANOR BRICKWORKS, THUNDERSLEY

Edward Corder, known as Ted, was born 19th October 1868 at Crouch Green, Castle Hedingham, the youngest of the three sons of Robert Corder (1833-1915) and Harriet Corder formerly Parr (1834-1899).

Upon leaving school, Ted worked with his father in the brickmaking industry at Brick Kiln Hill Brick Works at Castle Hedingham. In 1888, Ted, together with Richard Bingham and Arthur Finch all of Castle Hedingham, went to America to *"seek their fortunes"*. (1) Richard James Bingham, born circa 1868 was a son of Edward Bingham (1829-1916) the well known ornamental potter of Castle Hedingham who himself moved to America in 1906. Arthur Finch, born 1869, was a nephew of Mary Ann Finch (1840-1924) who in 1860 married James Corder (1840-1907), a younger brother of Ted's father Robert. Ted promised his parents he would return to England within six years and therefore came back in about 1894 and resumed work at the Brick Kiln Hill Brick Works, which were managed by his father.

By 1901 Ted became foreman of the Hedingham Brick and Tile Works at Highfield, Sible Hedingham, owned by Mark Gentry. Ted lived nearby at *"The Brick Kiln"* (now Alderford Farm), which was the former brickworks of the Hilton family. (2). Later in 1901 Ted became manager of The Manor Brickworks Limited at Thundersley, Essex and moved to New Thundersley. Towards the end of 1901 he married Alice Dyson (1864-1920), also a native of Castle Hedingham, at Castle Hedingham Chapel. They lived at The Manor, Thundersley, where their son Edward Dyson Corder, was born on 29th October 1902.

On 31st December 1902 plans were deposited with Rochford Rural District Council by Alfred T. Castle, architect and builder, of Iron Alvis, South Benfleet, on behalf of Edward Corder for erection of a new house and shed at Church Road, Thundersley. The plans were approved on 6th January 1903, which is very quick compared with current standards. The location was at the junction of Church Road with Hazlemere Road where Edward Corder had purchased a building plot with an 80 foot frontage and 150 foot length. Alfred Castle built the house for Edward Corder with 9 inch red brick work and red plain tiles manufactured at The Manor Brickworks Limited. (3) Edward and Alice Corder appropriately named their new house *'Hedingham House'*. Their daughter, Alice Muriel Gladys, was born at Hedingham House on 22nd September 1905.

On 11th December 1909 plans were approved by Rochford R.D.C., for a new bungalow at Hazlemere Road for Edward Corder. It was constructed by F. Sulman, builder, on a plot 100 feet wide and 160 feet long, with bricks and tiles supplied by The Manor Brickworks Limited. (4) The bungalow, named The Poplars, comprising of five rooms, was built as an investment. It was let to Henry Wheeler, whose son, Henry junior, was a labourer at The Manor Brickworks. In 1911 Edward's brother, John Corder (1863-1957) and his son Edward (1886-1938) were boarders at the bungalow, while both working as brick and tile makers at The Manor Brickworks. (5)

Hedingham House, New Thundersley, built for Edward Corder in 1903 with red bricks and tiles made at The Manor Brick Works. The house is located south east of the junction of Church Road with Hazlemere Road.

On 19th August 1905 a fire occurred at The Manor Brickworks, which was reported as follows:

> *"Destructive fire - A disastrous fire occurred on the night of the 19th ult. at New Thundersley, resulting in the loss of the buildings and machinery belonging to the Manor Brickfields Co. Everything was safe when the manager, Mr. Edward Corder, was there about 7 o'clock in the evening, but at about 8.25pm smoke was seen issuing from the shedding. The shedding, of which there was about 100 ft., contained some very valuable machinery and about 300,000 unfinished tiles. The loss is estimated at £1,200. Nothing could be done to stem the fierceness of the fire, which burned with great rapidity, fanned as it was by a very strong wind. The outbreak is believed to have been caused by a spark which was carried by the high wind from one of the kilns."* (6)

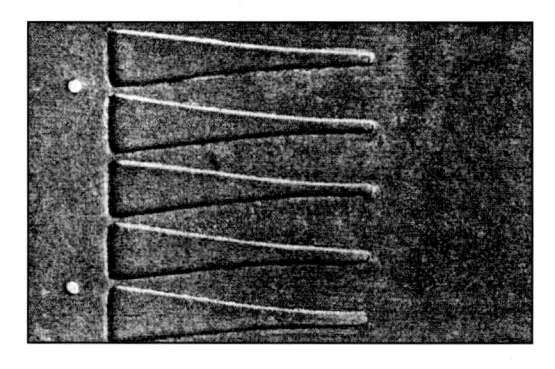

Roofing tile designed by Edward Corder for which he was granted a patent in 1909.

On 19th February 1909 Edward Corder and Cuthbert Edward Venables patented, *'Improvements in or relating to Roofing tiles and the like'* under patent no. 4,113. The new design of roofing tile was put on the market by the Manor Brickworks Limited. It had five shallow depressions of triangular shape, which extended nearly right across the upper part of the face of the tile just below the nailholes. These depressions got narrower as they approached the lower half of the tile, gradually shallowing until they terminated altogether at the point where the lower edge of the next overlapping tile came. They were therefore invisible where the tiles were fixed. These depressions were less than one eighth inch deep, but the horizontal part of them formed a most effective barrier against snow or rain reaching the nailholes or being driven over the top edge of the tile. Among the advantages for the use of these tiles was the following:

1. A saving in cost of materials and labour by the builder, as he was enabled to lay tiles to a 4.5 inch gauge instead of to a 4 inch gauge.
2. A saving of one-ninth of the total weight of the tiles and battens.
3. A saving of one-ninth of the time necessary to cover a roof with ordinary tiles.
4. A saving in cartage of materials.
5. A more weatherproof roof covering and one which prevented snow and rain from finding their way through the nailholes and over the top edge of the tiles.
6. A roof which did not retain the water between the tiles by capillary action - a frequent cause of their perishing through the lamination of their upper surface during a frost.
7. A roof which was easier to repair (having fewer parts)
   The new roofing tiles could be packed into the same space as ordinary tiles, as the ribs between the depressions did not project beyond the face of the tile.
   The Manor Brickworks Limited desired to find a firm of tile makers to take up the manufacture and sale of their patent roofing tile upon a royalty basis. (7)

In the 1911 census Edward Corder is recorded as *'Manager of Brickworks'* living at New Thundersley. (8) In about 1913 or 1914 he became postmaster and proprietor of The Post Office and Stores at Stanwell, Middlesex.

In 1915 Ted Corder volunteered for service in the First World War. It was not necessary for him to serve as he was too old and well over conscript age but he was anxious to do his bit for King and Country. He served in the Mechanical Transport Section of the Army Service Corps in the Cameroons, East Africa and later at Salonika in the Balkan campaign. He was badly injured when an armoured car he was driving took a direct hit from an artillery shell. He was found torn with shrapnel and half his stomach and a kidney missing. He was taken to hospital in Malta followed by convalescence in Chelsea, London. As a result of his injuries he was honourably discharged on 4th April 1918 His wife, Alice Corder, died at Hedingham House, Thundersley on 25th March 1920. After the First World War Ted purchased a dairy at Fleet, Hampshire. On 2nd January 1923 he married secondly, Gertrude Allen (1899-1980) in Darlington. In August 1923 they sailed to Canada with Alice Muriel Gladys Corder (1905-1987) who was Ted's daughter from his first marriage.

Ted purchased a 'Section' namely 640 acres of land (one square mile) known as *"The Old Service Ranch"* because it was formerly owned by Robert Service, the well known Canadian author and poet. Ted renamed it *"Darlington Ranch"*, which he farmed with both cattle and grain. In 1929 he sold *"Darlington Ranch"*, which was at Manville and moved to Vancouver Island and later to Gibson's Landing, British Columbia.

In November 1935 (Harry) Tucker Ripper, a Director of Rippers Limited of Castle Hedingham visited his old school friend, Edward Corder and gives a detailed description in his book. (9) Ted died on 20th November 1940 at Neepawa, Grantham's Landing, Howe Sound, British Columbia aged 72 years.

In 1926, Edward Dyson Corder (1902-1983) who had served in the Royal Navy in England followed his father to Canada and served for many years in the Canadian Navy. Three of his sons also joined the Canadian Navy, the eldest becoming a Captain. They are members of the ever increasing Corder family in Canada. (10)

Edward Corder (1868-1940) whilst serving in the Mechanical Transport Section of the Army Service Corps.

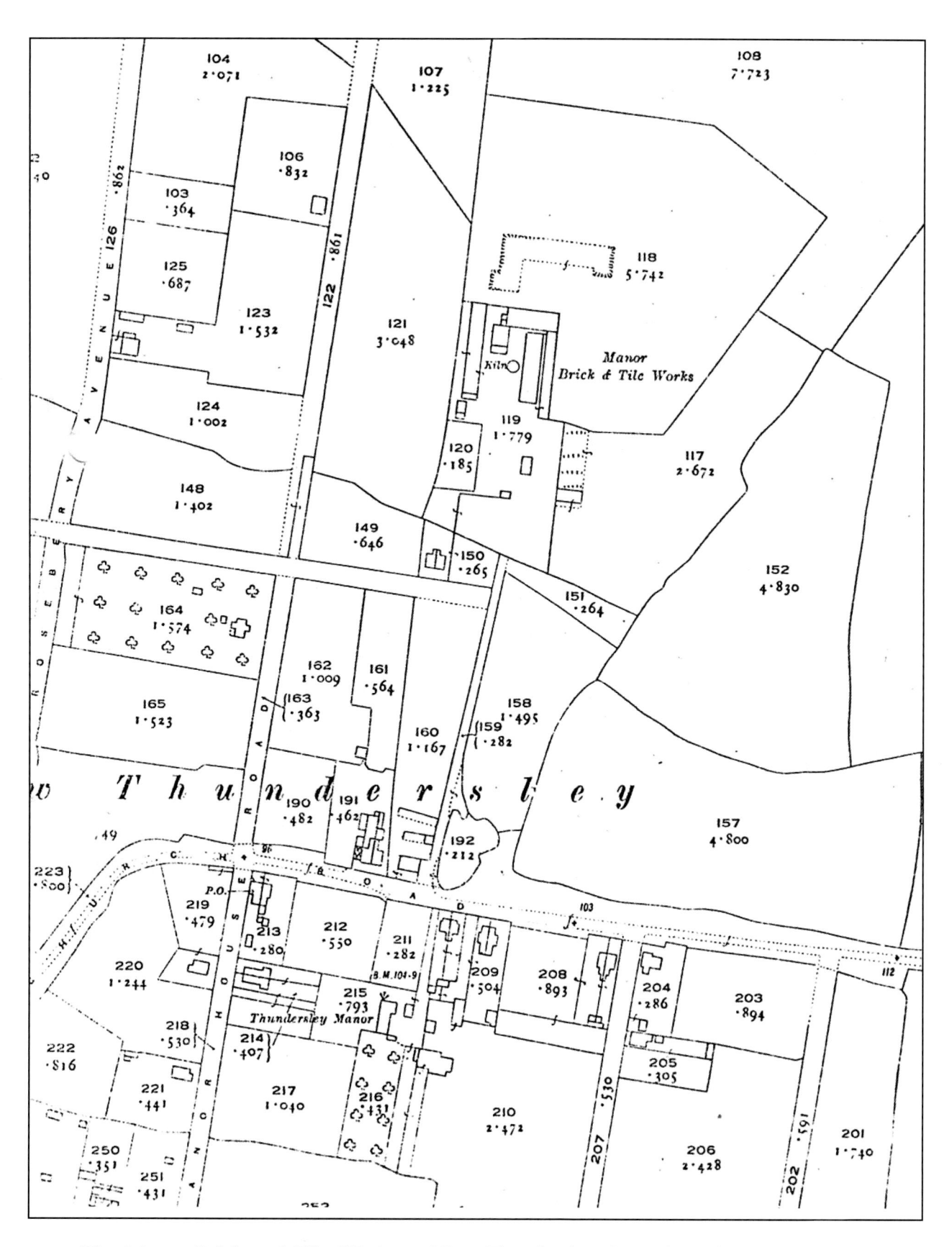

The Manor Brick and Tile Works at New Thundersley from the 25inch to one mile Ordnance Survey Map of 1923.

The Manor Brick Works at New Thundersley during the Edwardian era, when managed by Edward Corder. They are to the right of the tall trees where two chimneys from the downdraught kilns can be seen.

An enlargement of the above photograph showing The Manor Brick Works in its rural setting.

Chapter 13

DAVID CORDER (1837-1881), JAMES CORDER (1840-1907) AND ALFRED CORDER (1845-1898)

David Corder (1837-1881)

David Corder was the third son of John Corder (1806-1880). He was born at Gestingthorpe and baptised at Gestingthorpe Church on 11th June 1837. He followed his father and two elder brothers into the brickmaking industry being initially employed at Gestingthorpe until circa 1848 and thereafter at Brick Kiln Hill Brick Works, Castle Hedingham.

The 1851 census (1) records him as being employed as a *"Brick Maker"* at the age of 14 years. He probably continued as a brickmaker until about 1860 but does not appear to have moved with his parents from Crouch Green, Castle Hedingham, to Southey Green, Sible Hedingham. Unfortunately he cannot be found on the 1861 census but by 31st March 1864 when he married Elizabeth Hammond he was employed as a cellar-man in South Hackney. (2) Around 1867 he was a publican at Clerkenwell and later became proprietor of The Pine Apple, Blackfriars Road, Southwark. David and Elizabeth Corder had three children who all died young. Elizabeth predeceased her husband on 18th February 1873 and David died on 10th December 1881. (3)

Crouch Green, Castle Hedingham looking towards Great Yeldham. The cottages in the centre were occupied by the Corder family including David Corder when he was employed as a brickmaker at Brick Kiln Hill Brick Works.

James Corder (1840-1907)

James Corder was the fourth surviving son of John Corder (1806-1880). He was born at Gestingthorpe on 26th January 1840 and by 1851 when he was eleven years old he was employed as a brickmaker with his father and three elder brothers at Brick Kiln Hill Brick Works, Castle Hedingham. (4)

By the time of his marriage to Mary Ann Finch (1840-1924) on 30th October 1860 at Castle Hedingham Chapel he had ceased to be a brickmaker and was a wheelwright. (5) One of Mary Finch's elder brothers was Robert Finch, whose son Arthur, born 1869, joined Edward Corder (1868-1940) and Richard Bingham to go to Canada in 1888 to *"seek their fortunes"*. (6)

James Corder later became foreman carpenter for R. Hunt & Co. Limited, agricultural engineers, of Atlas Works, Earls Colne, where wooden patterns were made for the iron foundry. (7) In 1890 Zachariah Rogers, a builder and brickmaker of Earls Colne built a pair of houses for James Corder at Queens Road (then called New Road), Earls Colne for £248 0s 0d including labour and materials. These houses were known as *"Corder Villas"* and both were occupied by members of the family. James Corder died 26th August 1907 and by a sad coincidence his daughter in law, Annie Corder, died the same day. A double funeral took place, which aroused much sympathy in Earls Colne. (8)

James Corder is standing in the foreground of this photograph taken during or before 1902 in the wood and old pattern shop of R. Hunt & Co. Limited at Atlas Works, Earls Colne, where he was foreman carpenter for over thirty years.

Alfred Corder (1845-1898)

Alfred Corder was the sixth son of John Corder (1806-1880) and was born 28th January 1845 at Gestingthorpe. Alfred commenced work with his father and four surviving elder brothers at Brick Kiln Hill Brick Works, Castle Hedingham, during the mid 1850s. In about 1860 he moved with his parents to the Southey Green Brick, Tile and Pottery Works where he continued work in the brickmaking industry. On the 1861 census Alfred was recorded as a '*Brickmaker's Labourer*' (9) and was employed by his elder brother, William Corder (1835-1903).

Alfred Corder

By 1865 Alfred left the brickmaking industry and joined the building trade being employed by Robert Sudbury and Son, builders and contractors of Sudbury's Yard, Bridge Street, Halstead. During early June 1865 Sudbury and Son were erecting a large building on their own premises in which to carry on the manufacture of Ransomes patent stone, when a serious accident occurred. Several of the workmen were drinking beer on the scaffold about 22 feet high when the putlog against which they were leaning gave way and six of the men fell to the ground. One man escaped uninjured by grasping at a ladder standing nearby and sliding down it. The other men were severely cut and bruised particularly Alfred Corder but fortunately no bones were broken. (10) Alfred later became a stationery engine driver at Clovers Steam Flour Mills at Bridge Street, Halstead, where he worked for over thirty years. He died suddenly whilst at work in Clovers Mills on 22nd November 1898 aged 54 years. (11)

On 23rd July 1867 Alfred had married Mary Ann Norfolk Sudbury, sometimes recorded as Marianne (1844-1921), a daughter of Anthony Sudbury (1814-1876) and Amelia Sudbury nee Norfolk (1815-1889). (12) Alfred and Mary Ann Corder had seven children of whom one daughter, Margaret (1879-1940) married William James Wiseman, a brickmaker, in 1913. (13) (see chapter 16). Two sons were given the forename of Sudbury namely Frank Sudbury Corder (1870-1945) and Anthony Sudbury Corder (1881-1943). Anthony Sudbury was a master plasterer, bricklayer and builder who carried on his business from Bois Field and later from the Old Tan Yard, Halstead. The Sudbury family were engaged in the building industry for about one hundred years until the late 1920s when George Sudbury and Sons traded from Colchester Road, Halstead. (14)

The premises of George Sudbury & Sons, Builders and Undertakers at The Peaches, Colchester Road, Halstead in 1905. Following the death of George Sudbury (1829-1886) the business was continued by his sons, one of whom, Louis Sudbury (1859-1936), lived at The Peaches, now 38 Colchester Road.

Chapter 14

HENRY CORDER (1850-1934)

Henry Corder was born 18th December 1850 at Castle Hedingham and was known as Harry. He was the son of Eliza Corder (1830-1911) but was mainly brought up by his grandparents, John and Susan Corder. In about 1860 he moved with them from Crouch Green, Castle Hedingham to Southey Green, Sible Hedingham. In the 1861 census (1) he was recorded as a *'Brickmaker's Labourer'*, aged 10 years old. In the 1871 census (2) he was recorded as a *'Pot Maker'* (Potter) and in 1881 census (3) as a *'Potter (Earthenware Manufacturer)'*. The 1891 census (4) records him as a *'Pot Maker'* and 1901 census (5) as a *'Chimney Pot Maker (Earth-worker)'*. Throughout the majority of this time he was employed by his uncle, William Corder (1835-1903) at the Southey Green Brick, Tile and Pottery Works. William Corder was also proprietor of the Great Yeldham Brick, Tile and Pottery Works at Potters Hall, Great Yeldham during the 1890's, which Henry managed for his uncle for six years from 1892 until 1898. During these years Henry and his wife, Elizabeth, lived at Poole Street, Great Yeldham where their daughter, Laura (1893-1916) was born. (6)

In 1898 Henry, Elizabeth and Laura moved from Great Yeldham to the Old Tan Yard in Halstead and in 1901 to 30 Tidings Hill, Halstead, when Henry took over the business of a beer retailer. (7) He held the licence for well over 30 years, but his wife, Elizabeth, carried out much of the day to day running of the business. This was because Henry continued his work as a Potter until he was well over 70 years of age.

Following the death of his uncle William Corder, in 1903, Henry continued working for his cousin Harry Corder at the Southey Green Brick, Tile and Pottery Works until he retired in the early 1920s. The 1911 census records Henry as a *'Potter in the Brick and Pottery Industry'* living with his family at 30 Tidings Hill, Halstead. (8) Whilst working at Southey Green and living in Halstead, Henry walked to work each day via Broaks Wood. He used to get up at 4am, leave home at 5am to start work at 6am. He worked a 12 hour day until 6pm, walked home arriving at about 7pm and then helped his wife with their beer retailers business. During some months of the year Henry walked in darkness at both ends of the day!

Henry's speciality as a Potter was making large chimney pots, which were sometimes so large that he required a labourer, usually a boy, to turn the wheel for him. He also glazed pots, fired them and attended exhibitions, demonstrating pottery making. Occasionally, when there was insufficient work for him at Southey Green Brick, Tile and Pottery Works he worked as a Potter for one or two seasons (years) for each of the following brickmakers and potters:

    Pudney & Son at Colne Engaine
    W. H. Collier at Marks Tey
    Bryan & Son, Wood Street Potteries, Chelmsford (the Bryan family, like the Corder family, originated from Gestingthorpe).

It is interesting to note that when Henry retired as a Potter in the early 1920s he finished his working career at Southey Green where he had started work some sixty years earlier.

Until 1930, when he was in his 80th year, he worked part time for Adams Brewery at Trinity Street, Halstead when he found the work in the brewery much *"lighter"* than in the brickworks and potteries. Thereafter he continued running his off licence until his death in 1934 at the age of 83 years. (9)

Henry Corder

Descendants of Eliza Corder   ***Descendants of Isaac Boreham***

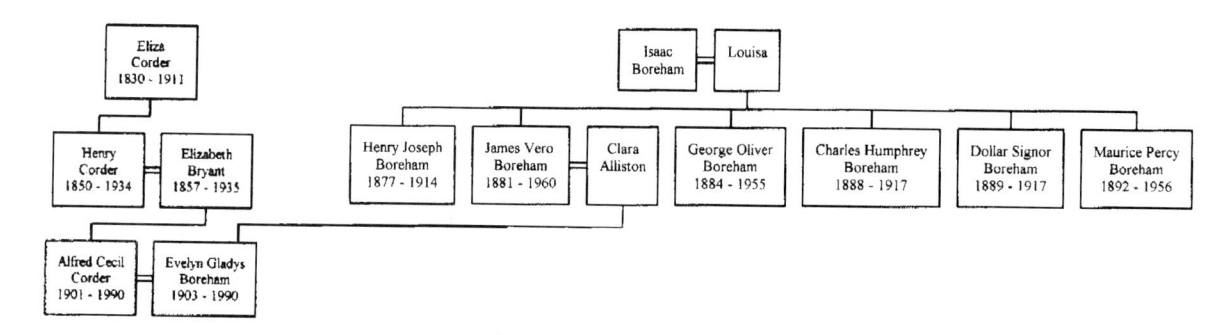

(For further information see chapter 16)

Chapter 15

RELATED BRICKMAKING FAMILY FROM CASTLE HEDINGHAM

Samuel Westrop (1830-1867) and Alfred Westrop (1853-1879)

The Westrop family was large and well known in Castle Hedingham. Samuel Westrop (1830-1867) was a brickmaker working at Brick Kiln Hill Brick Works, Castle Hedingham when it was managed by his father in law, John Corder (1806-1880). Samuel married Eliza Corder (1830-1911) in 1853 and they had seven children. The eldest son, Alfred Westrop, was born at Castle Hedingham on 29th October 1853 and became a potter. Although Alfred was recorded as a *'straw plaiter'* aged 7 years on the 1861 census (1) he soon followed his father and maternal grandfather into the clayworking industry. By the time of the 1871 census (2) when Alfred was 16 years of age he was recorded as a *'pot maker'* (potter) living with his grandparents at Southey Green Brick, Tile and Pottery Works. He was employed by his uncle William Corder (1835-1903) for a few years. Alfred later moved to London where he lived with his widowed mother and younger siblings. He died at 47 Clayhall Road, Bow on 9th September 1879 aged 26 years. (3)

The site of the former brickworks at Brick Kiln Hill, Castle Hedingham, where Samuel Westrop was employed as a brickmaker. Following closure during the early 1900s the buildings were removed but some of the clay pits survive as shown in this view photographed by the author in 1985.

Brick Kiln Hill Brick Works, Castle Hedingham, shown on the map which accompanied the sale catalogue of the Hedingham Castle Estate 1893. The Vendor was James Henry Alexander Majendie. The brickworks was situated on Nunnery Farm, which then formed part of the Castle Estate. The freehold of Nunnery Farm was later sold to James Mayhew Balls who was the tenant. Thomas Moy remained as tenant of the brickworks. The remainder of the Castle Estate was not sold in 1893 and was again advertised for sale in 1896 but no purchaser was found and the estate remained in the ownership of the Majendie family. Robert Corder who managed these brickworks for Thomas Moy lived in a cottage at Crouch Green (plot no. 273). The map shows a clay pit in the northern part of field 279 (east of the railway and south of the river) where white clay was dug for Edward Bingham's ornamental pottery. (Reproduced by courtesy of Essex Record Office, ref: Sale Cat. 1071).

Chapter 16

RELATED BRICKMAKING FAMILIES FROM SIBLE HEDINGHAM

Boreham family

The Boreham family were related to the Corder family through the marriage of Alfred Cecil Corder (1901-1990) to Evelyn Gladys Boreham (1903-1990) on 24th December 1933. (1)   Gladys, as she was known, was a daughter of James Vero Boreham, known as Vero, who was employed as a brickmaker in Sible Hedingham, when his average pay was 15/- a week. Sometime after the First World War he became foreman of a brickfield at Hatfield, Hertfordshire.

He was one of six sons of Isaac and Louisa Boreham of Hill House, Cobbs Fenn, Sible Hedingham, who were also the parents of six daughters.   All six sons served in the First World War and three of them lost their lives.   A contemporary newspaper report stated that this family was *"doing its bit"*. (2)   Three of Vero's brothers were also employed as brickmakers in Sible Hedingham namely Henry Joseph, George Oliver and Charles Humphrey.   Henry Joseph, known as Harry, was variously recorded as a general labourer in a brickworks, a brickmaker and a ganger.   He later served in the Essex Regiment and was killed in action; Charles of the Middlesex Regiment died from his wounds on 8th May 1917. Another brother, Dollar Signor Boreham of the Northamptonshire Regiment was killed in action on 6th March 1917. (3)   Apart from Vero the surviving brothers were George and Percy.   The four brothers who were brickmakers prior to the First World War, were employed by Mark Gentry who owned the Langthorne Brick Works at Wethersfield Road and Highfield Brick Works near Purls Hill, Sible Hedingham.   George Oliver Boreham, known as Oliver, was recorded on the 1911 census as a *'brickmaker'*. (4)

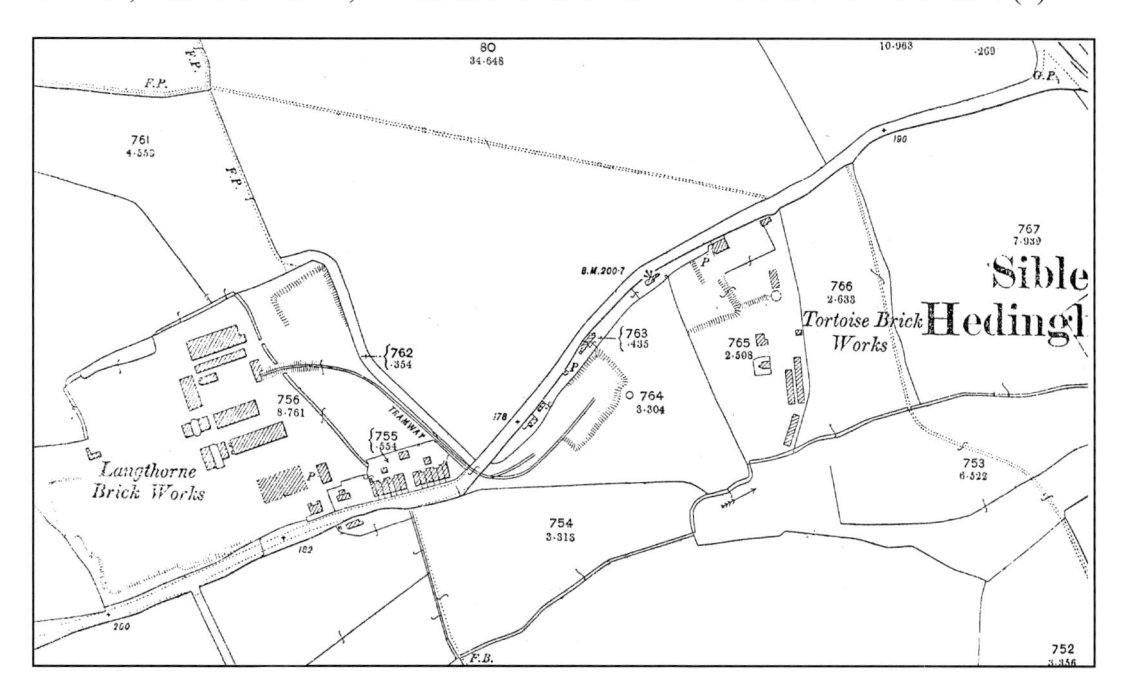

The Langthorne Brick Works of Mark Gentry and The Tortoise Brick Works of Eli Cornish from the 1897 Ordnance Survey Map of 25 inches to one mile scale.

Charles Humphrey Boreham (1888-1917) known as Humphrey, was a brickmaker at Mark Gentry's Highfield Brick Works. He is in a brickmaker's shed about to remove a 'green' brick from a mould and place it on a pallet board on a cradle barrow.

Brett, King and Gepp families

The Brett family of Sible Hedingham were related to the Corder family through the marriage of John Corder (1863-1957) to Alice Agnes Brett (1863-1951) on 9th May 1884 at Castle Hedingham Chapel.

Alice was a daughter of John and Eliza Brett. Two of their sons were employed in the brickmaking industry namely John Brett (1871-1938) and Robert Brett (1874-1944). They were both employed by the Rayner family at Maiden Ley Brick Works, Castle Hedingham. In 1901 John was a *'Brick Yard Labourer'* living in Alderford Street and later moved to Swan Street. In the 1901 and 1911 censuses Robert was recorded as a *'Brickmaker'* living in New England, Sible Hedingham.

In June 1910 Robert Brett was one of a party of fifty people who visited Germany to enquire into the questions of unemployment. The visit was arranged by the Tariff Reform League. (5)

On 4th March 1912 an accident occurred to Robert Brett, who had been a brickmaker in the employ of the Rayner family for sixteen years. The accident happened whilst several men were falling earth. The earth was being cut at the top and Robert was loading a barrow underneath. He was stooping in between a plank and the barrow when the earth fell over him. He tried to stand up to get clear of the fall, but was twisted onto his left side and the earth that fell came up to his knees. About a ton of earth fell from a height of about fourteen feet. The earth was pulled away but it was not clear whether it was the earth or plank that injured his back, as the plank was broken over the top of him. As well as injuring his back, he was also injured internally, was totally incapacitated and unable to follow his original occupation as a brickmaker. However he was later able to do some light work in other employment. He brought a claim under the Workmen's Compensation Act, which was heard at Halstead County Court on 26th May 1913 before His Honour Judge Tindal Atkinson. The claim was for 10/- a week but after long legal argument between Counsel and His Honour, judgment was given for 5/- a week. (6)

One of Alice Brett's sisters, Elizabeth Brett (1870-1945) married Arthur Downs (1870-1954). Sadly their two sons were killed during the First World War namely Harry Arthur Downs (1893-1918) and Charles Downs (1896-1916) who are commemorated on the Castle Hedingham War Memorial. Arthur was a first cousin to Harry, John and Fred Corder of Southey Green. One of Arthur's sisters, Emma (1875-1964) married Arthur George King (1873-1923) in 1897. At the time of his marriage Arthur King was a brickyard labourer and later became a market gardener on his own account. One of his brothers, Frederick Charles, was also a brickyard labourer when he married Ellen Finch in 1901 and is so recorded on the 1901 census. (7) Arthur and Emma King's eldest daughter, Gracie May (1898-1929) married William Bernard Gepp (1900-1965) in 1922. His father and grandfather were both employed in the brickmaking industry. Joseph Charles Gepp (1880-1904) was a brickyard labourer upon his marriage to Jessie Earey in 1900 and also on the census the following year. (8) His widow later married James Henry Smith of Castle Hedingham who was also a brickyard labourer. In 1911 William Gepp was living with his grandparents, Joseph and Sarah at Alderford Hall, Sible Hedingham. (9) Joseph Gepp (1850-1930) was a brickmaker but with the seasonal nature of the work he was employed in maltings in Sible Hedingham during the winter months. He retired as a brickmaker and maltster in 1918 and continued living at Alderford Hall, which was the Gepp family home for over forty years. (10) Ernest Edward, another son of Joseph senior, was initially a brickmaker and was later employed by Rippers Limited for about fifty years. (11).

Descendants of John Brett

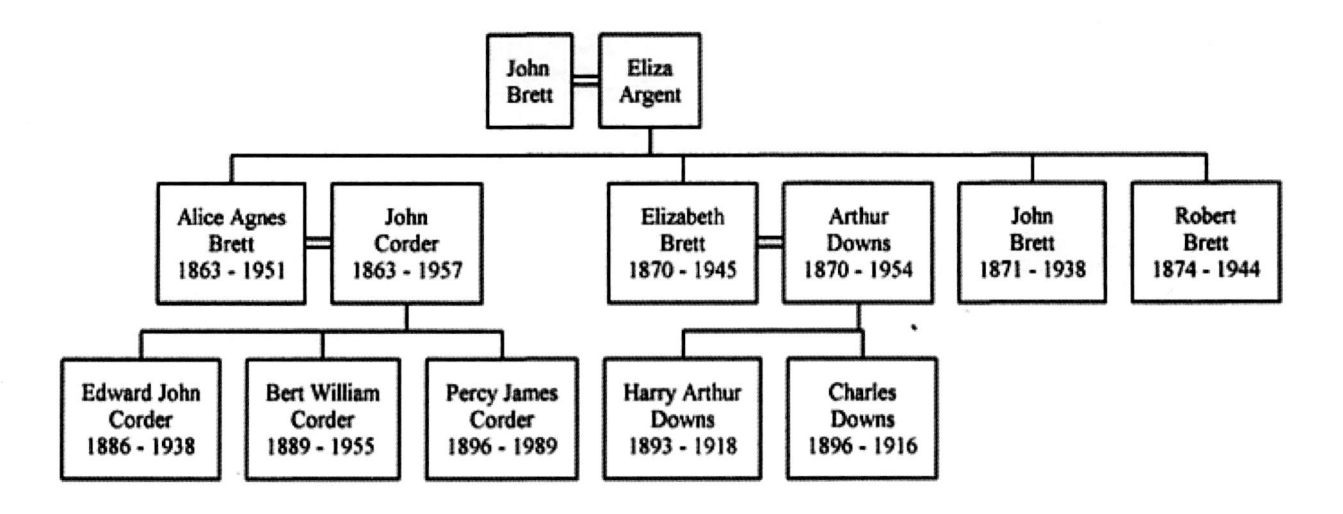

```
                        John ── Eliza
                        Brett   Argent
          ┌──────────────┬───────────┬──────────┬──────────┐
   Alice Agnes ── John        Elizabeth ── Arthur     John       Robert
     Brett      Corder          Brett      Downs      Brett      Brett
   1863-1951   1863-1957      1870-1945   1870-1954  1871-1938  1874-1944
   ┌────────┬────────┐           ┌────────┐
Edward John  Bert William  Percy James   Harry Arthur   Charles
  Corder      Corder        Corder         Downs        Downs
1886-1938   1889-1955     1896-1989      1893-1918    1896-1916
```

Descendants of William Downs

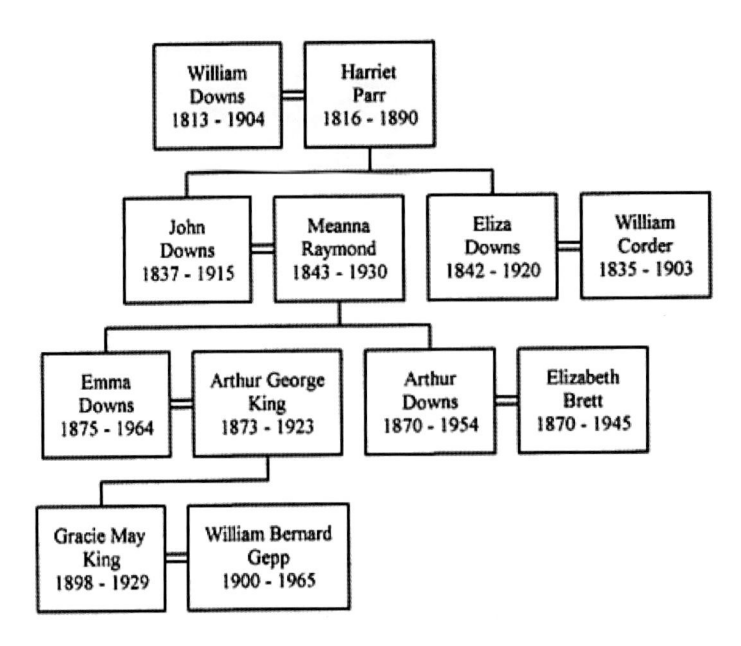

```
William Downs (1813-1904) — Harriet Parr (1816-1890)
    |
    ├── John Downs (1837-1915) — Meanna Raymond (1843-1930)
    ├── Eliza Downs (1842-1920) — William Corder (1835-1903)
        |
        ├── Emma Downs (1875-1964) — Arthur George King (1873-1923)
        ├── Arthur Downs (1870-1954) — Elizabeth Brett (1870-1945)
            |
            Gracie May King (1898-1929) — William Bernard Gepp (1900-1965)
```

Descendants of Joseph Gepp

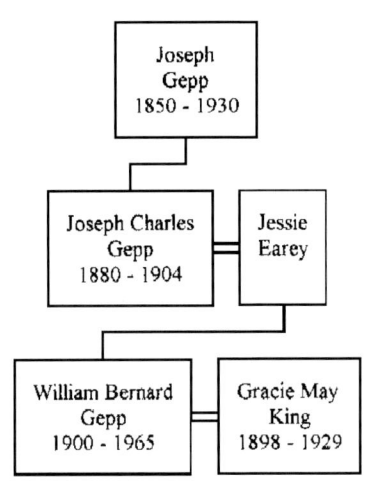

```
Joseph Gepp (1850-1930)
    |
    Joseph Charles Gepp (1880-1904) — Jessie Earey
        |
        William Bernard Gepp (1900-1965) — Gracie May King (1898-1929)
```

The Willett family

Daniel Willett (1837-1915) was a maltster of Malting Cottages, Queen Street, Sible Hedingham. He married Susanna Ann Smith (died 1899) and they had ten children. The eldest was Alice Ann (1861-1927) who married George Corder (1863-1938) in 1885.

One of Daniel and Susanna's sons was Harry Willett (1869-1950) who worked for William Corder at Gosfield Brick Works from 1890 until 1895 when it was under the management of George Corder (Harry's brother in law). From 1895 to 1939 Harry worked intermittently for William Corder and later for Harry Corder, at the Southey Green Brick, Tile and Pottery Works. The author's mother remembered Harry Willett working at Southey Green as a tile maker during the 1930's.

Descendants of Thomas Willett

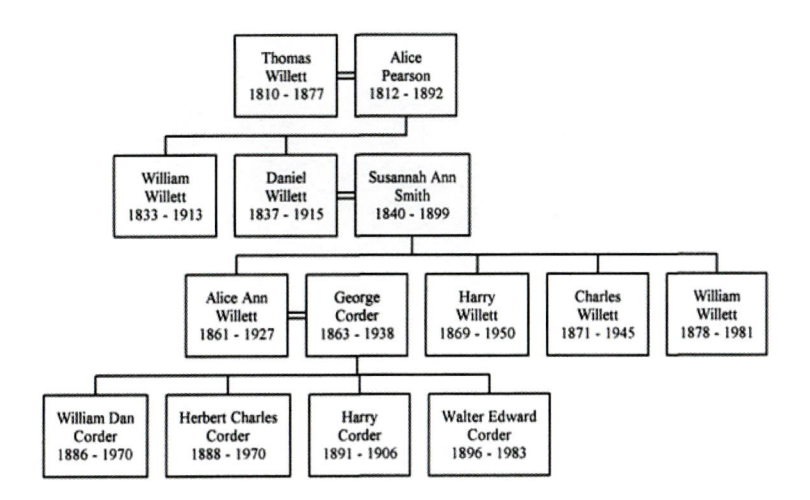

```
Thomas Willett 1810-1877 === Alice Pearson 1812-1892
    |
    ├── William Willett 1833-1913
    ├── Daniel Willett 1837-1915 === Susannah Ann Smith 1840-1899
    │       |
    │       ├── Alice Ann Willett 1861-1927
    │       ├── George Corder 1863-1938
    │       │       |
    │       │       ├── William Dan Corder 1886-1970
    │       │       ├── Herbert Charles Corder 1888-1970
    │       │       ├── Harry Corder 1891-1906
    │       │       └── Walter Edward Corder 1896-1983
    │       ├── Harry Willett 1869-1950
    │       ├── Charles Willett 1871-1945
    │       └── William Willett 1878-1981
```

Two other sons of Daniel and Susanna Willett namely Charles (1871-1945) and William (1878-1981) were in partnership as coal merchants operating from a barn near Alderford Water Mill, Alderford Street, Sible Hedingham. They supplied coal to Harry Corder's brickworks and pottery at Southey Green for many years until 1939. Following the death of Charles in 1945, William became sole proprietor. In July 1947 William sold his coal merchants business to Thomas Moy Limited and lived to the grand old age of 103 years.

Walter Edward Corder (1896-1983) with his uncle William Willett (1878-1981). This photograph was taken by the author at Black Notley Hospital in July 1979 upon the occasion of Williams 101st birthday. Thereafter he lived for another two years four months becoming the oldest native of Sible Hedingham.

William James Wiseman (1882-1959)

In 1913, William James Wiseman married Margaret Corder (1879-1940), a daughter of Alfred Corder (1845-1898). William, known as "Swagger" Wiseman, was employed in the brickmaking industry in the Hedinghams for the majority of his working life. In the 1901 census (12) at the age of 18 years he is recorded as a *"Brickmaker"* and similarly in the 1911 census (13) he is also recorded as a *"Brickmaker"* when employed by Mark Gentry at his Langthorne Brick Works.

When this Brick Works closed in 1911, William found employment at Maiden Ley Brick Works, Castle Hedingham for the Rayner family, with the exception of the Second World War years. This was because their brickworks had up draught kilns, which could not operate owing to the blackout restrictions and the likelihood of enemy pilots seeing the fires. William then found employment with Rippers Limited, either in their joinery works or at their subsidiary company, The Sible Hedingham Red Brick Company Limited, which was able to operate during the war because their down draught kilns could be adequately covered so enemy pilots could not see the fires. He returned to Rayners Brick Works after the war and retired in 1948. He died on 29th April 1959 aged 76 years and was buried in Castle Hedingham Cemetery (14).

An engine called *'The Tin Pot'* and trucks at Langthorne Brick Works circa 1905 used to haul clay from the pits on one side of Wethersfield Road to the brickworks owned by Mark Gentry on the other. The driver of the engine was 'Bunny' Beadle and two of the other men are Harry 'Higgler' Broyd and William James 'Swagger' Wiseman.

Chapter 17

RELATED BRICKMAKING FAMILIES FROM GESTINGTHORPE

The Finch family

Thomas Finch (1833-1932) of Gestingthorpe, known as 'Old Tom Finch' had three sons who were employed as brick and tile makers by the Rayner family in Gestingthorpe at various times.

The eldest son was Arthur William Finch (1864-1943), known as "Potty" Finch because he made pottery. He was also the head kiln man and burner. His son Alfred Thomas (1883-1944) was a tile maker and Alfred's son, Albert Arthur (1909-1974) was also a tile maker. As well as working for the Rayner family at Gestingthorpe, Albert also worked for Harry Corder at the Southey Green Brick, Tile and Pottery Works as a tilemaker for a few years during the mid to late 1930s. Alfred's younger brother was George Barnabas Finch (1895-1991), known as "Rover" Finch because he was *"always chasing about"*. During the early 1900s he did an hours work at Rayner's brickyard before and after school, every day, to help an uncle who was a tilemaker. It was Rover's job to put the 'green' tiles in the 'loca' or 'drying shed'.

Up draught kiln at Rayner's Brick Works at the Clamp, Gestingthorpe sometime prior to 1915. Left to right: Frank Surridge, George Henry Finch, …… Finch, Ernie Turner, Thomas Ezekiel Finch and Edward Benjamin Finch. The man standing in the entrance to the kiln is Arthur William Finch, the head kiln man and burner.

The second son was George Henry Finch (1867-1955) who married Edith Corder (1864-1944) in 1886 and they had five children. George was employed by the Rayner family in Gestingthorpe as a tilemaker for many years. Their son, Edward Benjamin (1886-1918) was also a tilemaker at Gestingthorpe.

The third son was Alfred Benjamin Finch (1870-1945), a brick and tile maker, who also made pamments. He married Myra Corder (1868-1920) a sister of Edith Corder, in 1887. Myra who was born in 1868 at Gestingthorpe, was a daughter of Ezekiel Thomas Corder (1842-1897) by his first wife, Mary Ann Corder nee Ives (1841-1874). Myra was the only known female member of the Corder family to be employed in the brickmaking industry. Alfred and Myra had ten children between 1888 and 1910. After her marriage she worked in the Gestingthorpe Brick Works and combined work with running a house and bringing up ten children. It was not uncommon for a husband and wife to make bricks and tiles and to engage their children as labourers. The children would place the pug on their parents making tables and remove the 'green' bricks onto a cradle barrow and sand them if necessary. An adult, usually the wife, would wheel the barrow (known as 'bearing-off') to the hacks and the children would empty the barrow and return it. As the 'green' bricks dried, the children would 'skintle' them; that is turn them round so that the sun could reach and dry all sides. In such family situations it was often only the husband who was paid. He was paid piece work of so much a thousand, so the more he made, the greater the family income. Therefore if his wife and children helped him as his labourers, he could make more bricks and tiles and increase the family income. It was inevitable that at least three of Alfred and Myra's sons were associated with the brick and tile making industry in Gestingthorpe:

Thomas Ezekiel (1889-1919) became a brick and tile maker, prior to service as a Gunner in the Royal Field Artillery during the First World War. At the end of hostilities he returned to Gestingthorpe and resumed work as a brickmaker but died of Phthisis at his home on 5th July 1919 aged 30 years. (1)

George Frederick (1894-1976) was a carter's man and his work included transporting bricks and tiles from Rayners Brickworks by horses and cart prior to the First World War. (2) He was wounded whilst serving in the 10th Essex Regiment and in 1918 married Lilian Lebeau in Gestingthorpe Church. Her brother, Henry Edwin Lebeau (1897-1917) who had previously worked for George English, the brickmaker and farmer of Bulmer, became a stretcher bearer in the Royal Army Medical Corps and was killed in action on 2nd November 1917. (3) The Lebeau family lived in Pot Kiln Chase, Gestingthorpe.

Arthur John (1910-1992), known as Dick Finch, became a brickmaker and later a farm worker. When interviewed by Ashley Cooper he stated,

"I can remember when there were at least twelve men working at Rayner's brickyard here (Gestingthorpe) - and do you know - at least seven of them were Finches! But my father didn't only make bricks. He also made tiles. And that's a lot more skilful! The other thing he made were 'pamments' - and they were a foot square. Now father was a strong man - but you wanted to be strong to do that job! The thirst he worked up! Cuh! He drank enough beer to float the Queen Mary on! The sweat just ran off him! But every single time I go past 'Long Acre' (near the Pheasant), I think to myself, 'my father made all the bricks in that house - and ol' Ernie Taylor made all the tiles!"

Bricks were made on 'piece-work', Dick Finch explains,

> "When I left school my father was paid 8/3d for every 1,000 bricks. It makes you wonder really. People would work like hell from 6am to 6pm to get a shilling a day more than farm-workers."
>
> "Every winter, all the unskilled chaps were stood off. Eventually we might get a little 'dole' money - but even then we had to 'sign on' three times a week!"
>
> "And talk of a struggle! I've dug sand out of one end of Delvyns Pit. But we hadn't got any Wellington boots that time of day and the bloomin' water ran in almost as fast as we dug the sand out! In fact it's the only time I can remember them 'finding' us beer. But there was one benefit. If we were digging clay we could keep different types separate. The very best 'red' clay was used for ridge tiles. And the white clay from the 'bottom yard' here, was so good that they actually used to take it to Bulmer Brickyard - by horse and tumbril!" (4)

Albert Arthur Finch and Arthur John (Dick) Finch at Rayner's Brick Works, Gestingthorpe circa early 1930s. Dick Finch married Ruby Florence Rippingale (1919-1992) whose father, Arthur Rippingale (1884-1966) was a brickmaker in his younger days. In 1931 Dick's wages as a brickmaker were about thirty shillings a week. He was in regular work in the summer but not in the winter. (5)

Barnard Alfred Finch (1905-1975), another son of Alfred and Myra, said of his father, who worked in the Gestingthorpe Brick Works for the majority of his working life from 6am to 6pm:

> "He worked so hard you could see a lather of sweat round the big leather belt he wore, like a horse with sweat.. He used to say 'The work I've done, you'd've all been millionaires, if I'd been paid right'". (4)

Thomas Corder (1769-1841) who appears in the family tree on page 12 had a younger son Edward Corder (1818-1896), who was the father of Ezekiel Thomas Corder (1842-1897). Ezekiel had ten children of whom four daughters, Edith, Myra, Mary Ann and Lily are included in the following family trees.

Descendants of Thomas Corder

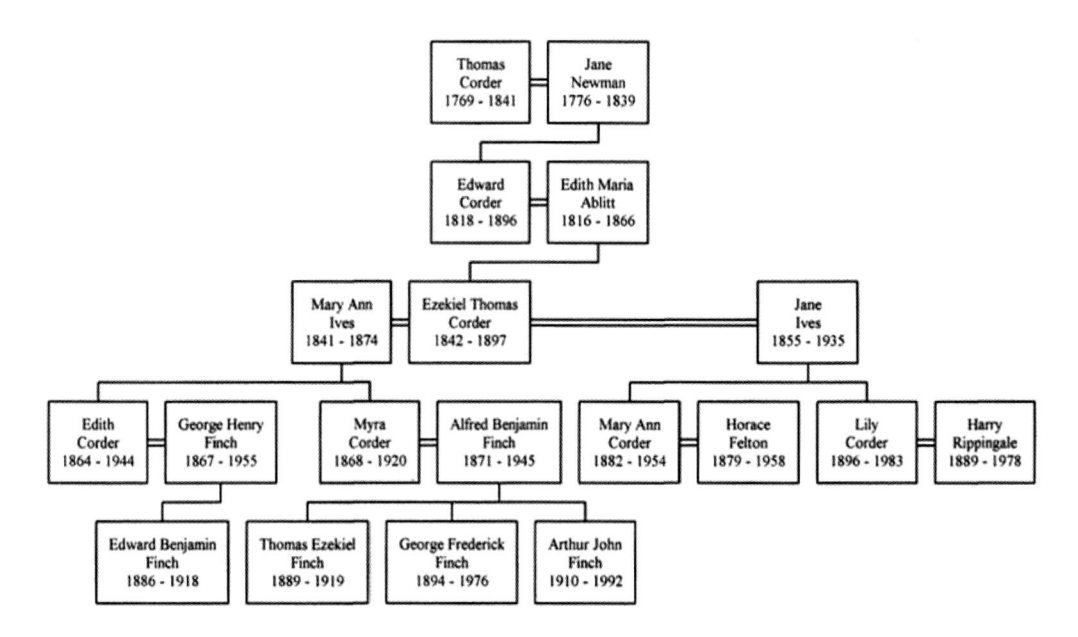

- Thomas Corder 1769 - 1841 = Jane Newman 1776 - 1839
  - Edward Corder 1818 - 1896 = Edith Maria Ablitt 1816 - 1866
    - Mary Ann Ives 1841 - 1874 = Ezekiel Thomas Corder 1842 - 1897 = Jane Ives 1855 - 1935
      - Edith Corder 1864 - 1944 = George Henry Finch 1867 - 1955
      - Myra Corder 1868 - 1920 = Alfred Benjamin Finch 1871 - 1945
        - Edward Benjamin Finch 1886 - 1918
        - Thomas Ezekiel Finch 1889 - 1919
        - George Frederick Finch 1894 - 1976
        - Arthur John Finch 1910 - 1992
      - Mary Ann Corder 1882 - 1954 = Horace Felton 1879 - 1958
      - Lily Corder 1896 - 1983 = Harry Rippingale 1889 - 1978

Descendants of Thomas Finch

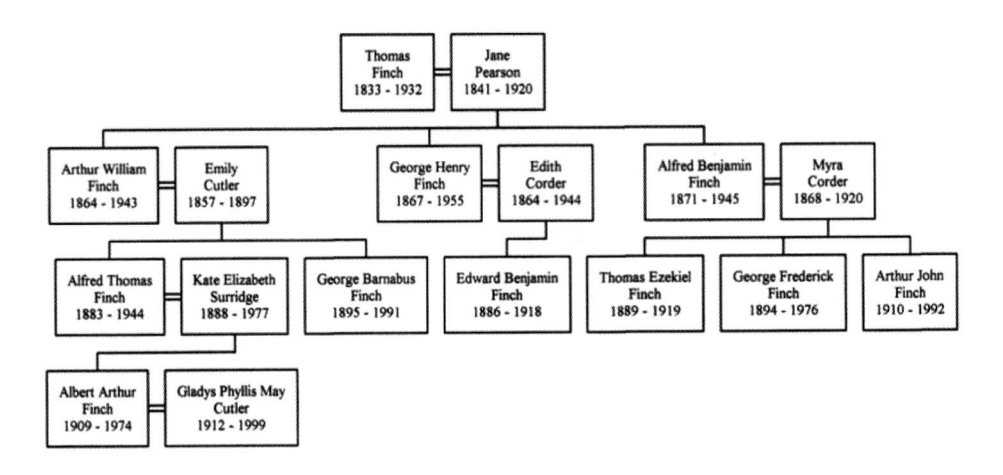

- Thomas Finch 1833 - 1932 = Jane Pearson 1841 - 1920
  - Arthur William Finch 1864 - 1943 = Emily Cutler 1857 - 1897
    - Alfred Thomas Finch 1883 - 1944 = Kate Elizabeth Surridge 1888 - 1977
      - Albert Arthur Finch 1909 - 1974 = Gladys Phyllis May Cutler 1912 - 1999
    - George Barnabus Finch 1895 - 1991
  - George Henry Finch 1867 - 1955 = Edith Corder 1864 - 1944
    - Edward Benjamin Finch 1886 - 1918
  - Alfred Benjamin Finch 1871 - 1945 = Myra Corder 1868 - 1920
    - Thomas Ezekiel Finch 1889 - 1919
    - George Frederick Finch 1894 - 1976
    - Arthur John Finch 1910 - 1992

Descendants of Walter Rippingale

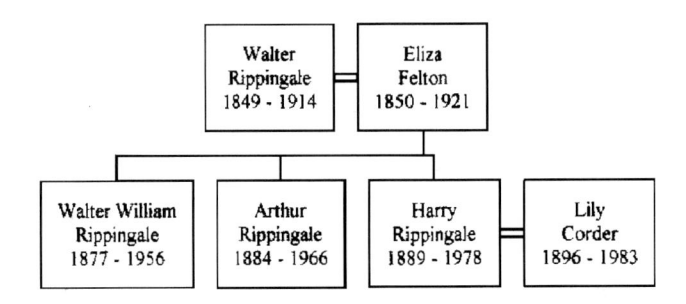

- Walter Rippingale 1849 - 1914 = Eliza Felton 1850 - 1921
  - Walter William Rippingale 1877 - 1956
  - Arthur Rippingale 1884 - 1966
  - Harry Rippingale 1889 - 1978 = Lily Corder 1896 - 1983

The Felton family of Gestingthorpe

Horace Felton (1879-1958), a son of Alfred and Mary Felton nee: Finch, of Brickyard Lane, Gestingthorpe, married Mary Ann Corder, known as Polly (1882-1954) in 1913. Horace was initially an agricultural labourer but was later employed by George English at his brickworks in Bulmer. Horace and Polly lived for some years in London but in 1929 returned to Gestingthorpe where they lived at Ellis Farm. (6)

Digging clay by hand at Bulmer Brick Works during the early 1900s. Horace Felton (1880-1958) is on the right.

Two of Horace's brothers were employed at Rayner's Brickworks in Gestingthorpe, namely Arthur and Walter who were both recorded in the 1911 census as *'Brickyard Labourers'*. (7) Arthur served in the 12th Suffolk Regiment during the First World War. Walter Felton (1893-1917) became a tilemaker for Rayners before enlisting into the Essex Regiment. He was later transferred to the Machine Gun Corps and was reported as missing on 3rd May 1917. Some time later his body was found with head and leg wounds and it was thought that he was killed instantaneously. It was not until late August 1917 that news of Walter's fate was received by his family in Gestingthorpe. The following month news arrived that William Corder (1889-1917) who was Polly Felton's brother was killed in action on 14th September 1917. A contemporary press report stated:

> *"The parish of Gestingthorpe is paying a heavy toll in the present war. Two more of the young men of the village have made the great sacrifice, viz., Pte. W. Corder, who was a gunner in a Siege Battery of the Royal Garrison Artillery and Pte. W. Felton of the Machine Gun Corps .... Mr. & Mrs. Felton who live in Brickyard Lane, only a few yards from Mrs. Corder, have lost two sons in the war and have two more sons serving. .... Previous to enlisting he (Walter Felton) was employed at Messrs. Rayner's Brickworks as a tile maker................"* (8)

Their brother Harry (1891-1916) of the 11th Essex Regiment was killed in action on 4th February 1916. Another brother also served in the First World War and survived.

The loss of brick and tile makers from Gestingthorpe, Sible Hedingham and elsewhere during the First World War contributed to a lack of skilled craftsmen when the brick, tile and pottery works re-opened in 1919.

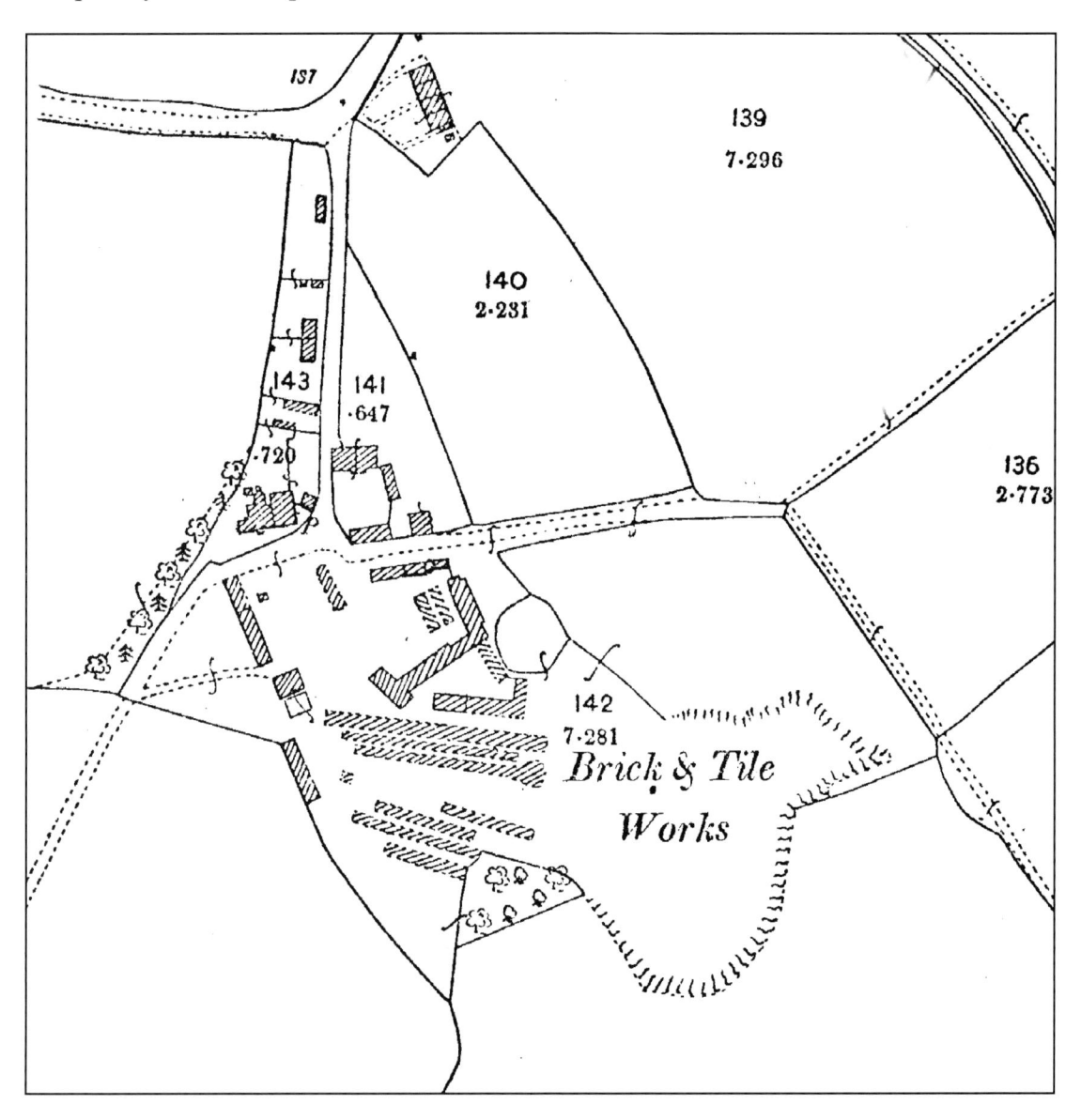

Rayner's Brick and Tile Works off Pot Kiln Chase, Gestingthorpe from the 1897 Ordnance Survey Map of 25 inches to one mile.

The Rippingale family and Harry Rippingale (1889-1978)

The Rippingale family is one of the oldest in Gestingthorpe. In the second half of the eighteenth century, Joseph Rippingale (1730-1807) was making pottery in the village and at least four of his harvest-pitchers survive. One is inscribed "*Joseph Reppingel 1767 Guesting Thorpe Essex*" and another is dated 1770. His second wife, who he married in 1766, was Mary Rayner of the brick and tilemaking family. (9) One of their sons was Samuel Rippingale, born 1767, who married Hannah Smith. Their son, Smith Rippingale (1789-1869) was born at Gestingthorpe where he learnt the craft of brickmaking. By the 1830's he was proprietor of Moulsham Brick Works, High Street, Moulsham, Chelmsford. (10) In 1841 (11) he was recorded as a '*brickmaker*' at High Street, Moulsham, in 1851 (12) at St. John's Road and in 1861 (13) at Lower Anchor Street, Chelmsford.

Harry Rippingale (1889-1978)

Harry Rippingale was born 29th September 1889 at Wisborough Hill, Gestingthorpe, the youngest of three sons of Walter Rippingale (1849-1914) by his second wife, Eliza Rippingale formerly Felton (1850-1921).

Walter was a pipe and tilemaker at Bulmer Brick and Tile Works for George English (1842-1920). When Harry was 12 years of age he left school and started work in the brickyard with his father and elder brothers earning 2/6d for a 59 hour week (about one old ha' penny an hour). On Sundays he used to feed the pigs for George English for which he was paid an extra three pence and given a rice pudding. There were 13 or 14 working in the yard then (c1901-1902) and they made large quantities of plain tiles. One man in the Edwardian period would make 1,200 bricks a day by hand if *"another chap did the grinding of the pug for three brickmakers a making at their tables"* (14) Some of the bricks, tiles and pipes were taken by horse and cart to Sudbury and Hedingham Railway Stations for transportation. At 17 years of age Harry was paid 7/6d a week and a man's rate was 12/- a week. Working hours for men were from 6am to 6pm and sometimes to 8pm except for Saturdays when they finished at 5pm. Whilst working for George English, Harry was sometimes required to work at Blackhouse Farm, Bulmer, which was previously owned by John Parmenter English (1845-1900), younger brother of George. Upon leaving George English at 17 years of age, Harry then worked with threshing tackle for six years for Billy Nott. During the First World War he worked in a munitions factory in Chelmsford when he regularly cycled between Gestingthorpe and Chelmsford.

Harry married Lily Corder (1896-1983) on 25th December 1924 at Gestingthorpe Church. (15) Lily was the youngest daughter of Ezekiel Thomas Corder (1842-1897) by his second wife Jane Ives (1855-1935). Jane's two elder brothers, Frederick and Robert Ives, were both employed as brickmakers at Ballingdon circa 1871. Lily helped Harry build up a number of business interests including omnibus proprietor, road haulage contractor, coal merchant, taxi, private car hire, petrol sales and farming including both arable and poultry with two thousand chickens.

After the First World War there was a decline in the use of horses and carts, barges, traction engines and to a certain extent in railways for transporting bricks, when lorries came into wider use. Harry was one of the first lorry proprietors in the area; he operated from his Garage at Audley End, Gestingthorpe. He purchased his first lorry, a one ton Model 'T' Ford from Stanley Downs of Sudbury for £170 in 1922. This lorry was used for hauling coal and bricks during the day. In the evening a bus body was lowered onto the vehicle by two pulleys, seats inserted and steps placed at the rear. It then carried 14 passengers and was the first omnibus to operate in the area. As a bus it was used by Harry to transport workers between Gestingthorpe and Courtauld's Mill in Halstead each morning and evening. The next morning the bus top, seats and steps were removed and the vehicle returned to its use as a lorry. He used the lorry for transporting bricks from Rayners Brick Works at Gestingthorpe to Sible and Castle Hedingham Railway Station and returned with coal to fire the kilns. He often made six round trips a day carrying bricks and coal and all the bricks had to be unloaded by hand into the railway trucks. He often worked 17 or 18 hours a day and did not employ anyone until six years after he started his business. (16)

In 1929 he purchased a Chevrolet (VX 435) in chassis form and built a lorry body onto it himself. By this time he had taken over an existing coal merchants business and used this lorry for delivering coal. In 1930 he needed another omnibus so he fitted a Lancia bus body onto this Chevrolet lorry. When the Traffic Commissioners came into being in 1930, they inspected this vehicle and found it suitable for public transport and commented that the conversion from lorry to bus was "a very good camouflage". Harry continued hauling bricks and coal until Rayners brickworks closed in 1951.

The Chevrolet lorry (VX 435) purchased by Harry Rippingale in 1929.

He sold his coach business in 1956 but continued his haulage and coal merchants business until he was in his 70s. By the 1970s he became acknowledged as the 'Grand Old Man of Omnibuses'. He continued his farming interests until his death on 5th October 1978 aged 89 years. (17)

Harry Rippingale's two elder brothers were also brickmakers in their younger working lives. The eldest brother, Walter William (1877-1956) was a brickmaker for much of his working life but also worked on the land in later life and resided at Wickham St. Paul. (18) The middle brother, Arthur (1884-1966) was also employed as a brickmaker and as a brickmaker's carter but later as a road worker. He is recorded on the 1911 census as a 'Brickmaker's Labourer'. (19) He married Kate Edith Martin (1884-1958) on 19th April 1909 at Gestingthorpe Church. Arthur and Kate lived successively at Wesbro Hills, The Barracks and New Cottages, Gestingthorpe. They had nine children including a daughter, Alice Lucy (1914-2007) who married Cecil Edward Corder (1913-1997) on 27th June 1936 in Gestingthorpe Church. They had three sons of whom the second son, Brian, born 1942, is the father of Raymond John Corder, born 1966, who was employed as a brickmaker at Bulmer Brick and Tile Works until 2008.

There was another Arthur Rippingale (1864-1940) who also lived at The Barracks in Gestingthorpe. He married Caroline Ives (1863-1949) in 1883. He was a horseman at Hill Farm, Gestingthorpe and in 1939 completed his 60th harvest when a photograph of him was published in the 'Farmer and Stock Breeder' magazine. Arthur and Caroline had seven children of which one son, Reginald Arthur (1900-1991) worked at Bulmer Brick Works circa 1931.

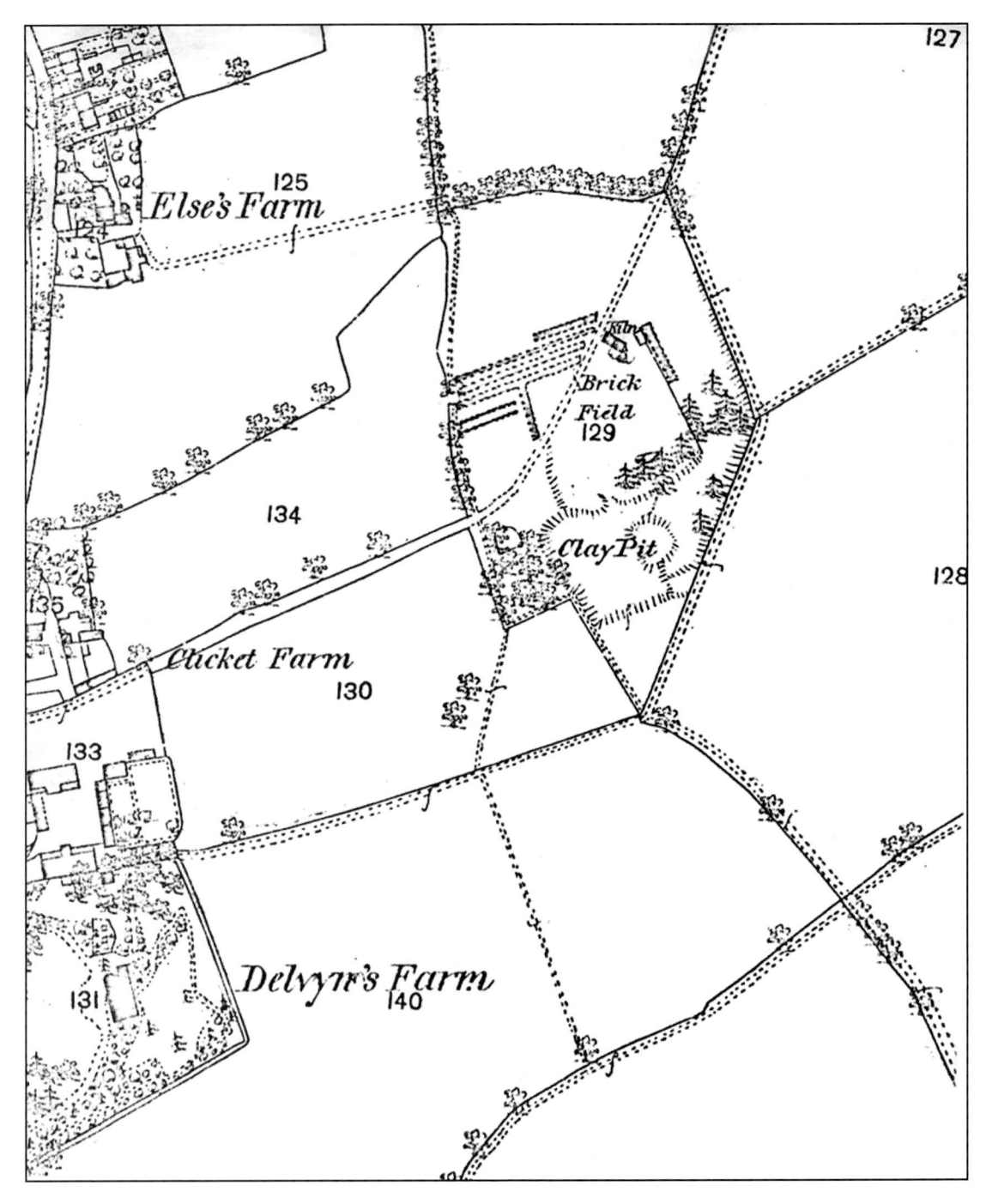

The Clamp or Upper Brick Works at Gestingthorpe from the 1876 edition of the Ordnance Survey Map of 25 inches to one mile.

Chapter 18

FINCH BRICK WORKS AT KINGSTON UPON HULL, YORKSHIRE

Interestingly, a completely different and more distant branch of our collateral ancestry owned two brickworks at Sutton and Marfleet, now within the Borough of Kingston upon Hull, Yorkshire, during the second quarter of the twentieth century.

Gascoin Foster Finch, born 28th April 1836 and George Finch (1838-1892) were the youngest sons of Richard Witty Finch (1805-1854). In 1851 the family was living in Trippett Street, Hull, when Gascoin, aged 14, was an apprentice joiner. (1) George later joined his elder brother as an apprentice joiner. Upon completing their apprenticeships, they both became joiners at Trippett Street by the late 1850s. Gascoin, with his wife and daughter, actually lived in Trippett Street (2) where Gascoin had his joinery workshop. George, with his wife and family lived successively at 5 Annies Place, off Charles Street, (3), Little Albion Street, 13 Liddell Street and finally at 44 Mason Street. George had a joinery workshop at Edward Street and by 1876 had returned to Trippett Street. (4)

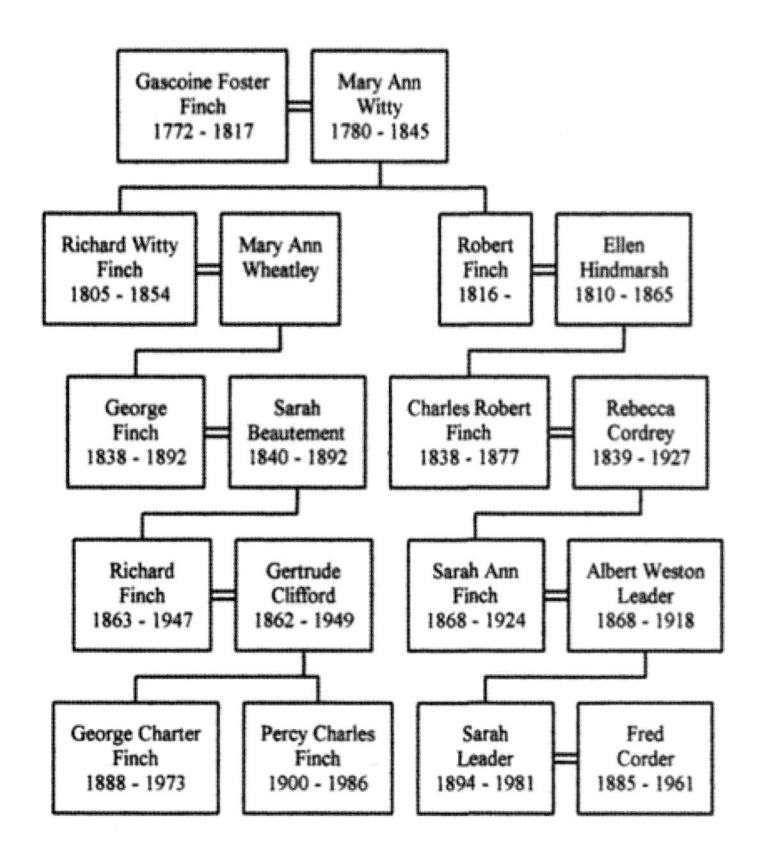

```
         Gascoine Foster  ══  Mary Ann
             Finch              Witty
           1772 - 1817        1780 - 1845
                  │
      ┌───────────┴───────────┐
  Richard Witty ══ Mary Ann     Robert  ══  Ellen
     Finch        Wheatley      Finch      Hindmarsh
   1805 - 1854                  1816 -     1810 - 1865
        │                              │
   George    ══  Sarah         Charles Robert ══ Rebecca
   Finch       Beautement         Finch          Cordrey
  1838 - 1892  1840 - 1892      1838 - 1877    1839 - 1927
        │                              │
   Richard  ══  Gertrude        Sarah Ann  ══  Albert Weston
   Finch        Clifford         Finch          Leader
  1863 - 1947  1862 - 1949     1868 - 1924    1868 - 1918
        │                              │
  George Charter ══ Percy Charles   Sarah  ══  Fred
     Finch            Finch         Leader    Corder
  1888 - 1973      1900 - 1986    1894 - 1981  1885 - 1961
```

George owned the freehold of the workshop, yard and premises at Trippett Street and extended his joinery business to include builders and undertakers. He died at his home at 44 Mason Street on 22nd May 1892 aged 53 years and for a short time his Executors continued the business. His Will and four Codicils gave his eldest son, Richard Finch (1863-1947), the option of purchasing the freehold property and fixtures at Trippett Street for £250 without any charge for goodwill but to exclude machinery, plant and tools. (5) Richard, who had worked for his father, accepted this option and continued trading.

George and Sarah's family of nine children included four sons. The second son, William Finch, A.S.I.R.P., born 1866, became a glazier, gasfitter, builder and contractor. He was an Associate of the Sanitary Institute of Great Britain and worked from 172 Beverley Road and later 2 Cave Street, Hull. Arthur (1875-1945), the youngest son, became a bricklayer at 54 New King Street, Hull and later a joiner. (6)

The eldest son, Richard, who continued his father's business, became a master builder, contractor, decorator and latterly a master brickmaker. He was a Fellow of the Institute of Builders and also a Baptist Preacher. He married Gertrude Clifford Charter (1862-1949) and they had three sons:
    George Charter Finch (1888-1973)
    Lawrence Richard Finch (1897-1903)
    Percy Charles Finch (1900-1986)
George became a builder, contractor and brick manufacturer whilst Percy was a builder, joinery contractor and Baptist Pastor.

TELEPHONE: 34268 CENTRAL.
R. FINCH (FELLOW INST. OF BUILDERS.)
JOINERY WORKS: TRIPPETT STREET,
HULL, Dec. 19th. 1927 192

To The Chairman of the Watch Committee,

RICHARD FINCH, SONS & CO.,
BUILDERS AND CONTRACTORS.

Dear Sirs,

    We estimate cost of Police Boxes according to detailed drawings at the sum of £42 - 10 - 0 each.

    Yours faithfully,

    p.p. R. Finch, Sons & Co.

    Geo. C. Finch

Letter from Richard Finch, Sons & Co., dated 1927 (Reproduced by courtesy of East Riding Archives and Local Studies ref: CCHU/2/4/8/4/44).

Richard initially traded on his own account and eventually took his two surviving sons into partnership trading as Richard Finch, Sons & Co. They continued trading at their joinery works at Trippett Street where Gascoin and George had started trading during the late 1850s. About eighty years later in 1938 a new company, R. Finch and Sons and Co. Limited, was incorporated with a capital of £5,000 in £1 shares and its registered office at 100 New Cleveland Street, Hull. (7) It appears that trading continued simultaneously at Trippett Street and at 100 New Cleveland Street (near its junction with Mulgrave Street).

In the late 1920s the first of two brick and tile works was acquired namely the Ings Road Brick Works at Ings Road, Sutton. This was followed by the acquisition of the Humber Brick Works at Hedon Road, Marfleet. (8) Apart from operating two brickworks the work as building contractors continued.

The original brickworks west of Lawrence Avenue and south of Clifford Avenue, both off the south of Ings Road, had become disused by 1927. A new brickworks was established on the north east side of Ings Road, which required a windpump to remove water from its clay pit.

The brickworks at Marfleet were originally operated by the Leonard family, who lived in Brickyard Cottage next to the Vicarage. By 1930 Thomas Herbert Leonard lived at The Grange Farm, also adjacent to the Vicarage in Church Lane. Their brickworks was north of St. Giles Church and east of the Vicarage, both north of Hedon Road and was the only brickworks in Marfleet. The bricks and tiles made here by the Leonard and later by the Finch families were used in much of the building in Marfleet during the first half of the twentieth century. (9)

On 19th December 1927 the partnership (as it then was) tendered for the erection of Police Boxes in Hull for £42 10s 0d each. The tender was successful and on 11th January 1928 a contract was entered into between Richard Finch trading as Richard Finch, Sons and Co and The Lord Mayor Aldermen and Citizens of Kingston upon Hull. (10)

By 1946, the company (as it became in 1938) of R. Finch & Sons & Co. Limited continued to operate the Ings Road Brick Works, but George Charter Finch was listed as proprietor of the Humber Brick Works at Hedon Road, Marfleet. (11) It appears that George Charter Finch operated the Brick Works, as he was described as a brick manufacturer, builder and contractor, whilst his brother Percy Charles Finch, was a builder and joinery contractor.

On 16th May 1949 the company entered into a contract with Yorkshire (East Riding) County Council for the erection of *"new out offices, alterations and additions"* to Easington County Primary School for £1,306 2s 11d. The directors were then Percy Finch and his wife Madeline May Finch (1896-1992). (12) The company continued as building contractors until 1957 or later.

The brickworks, latterly operated by George Charter Finch closed circa 1950's and the site of Ings Road Brickworks is now a school playing field. (13)

Humber Brick Works, Hedon Road, Marfleet in 1927.

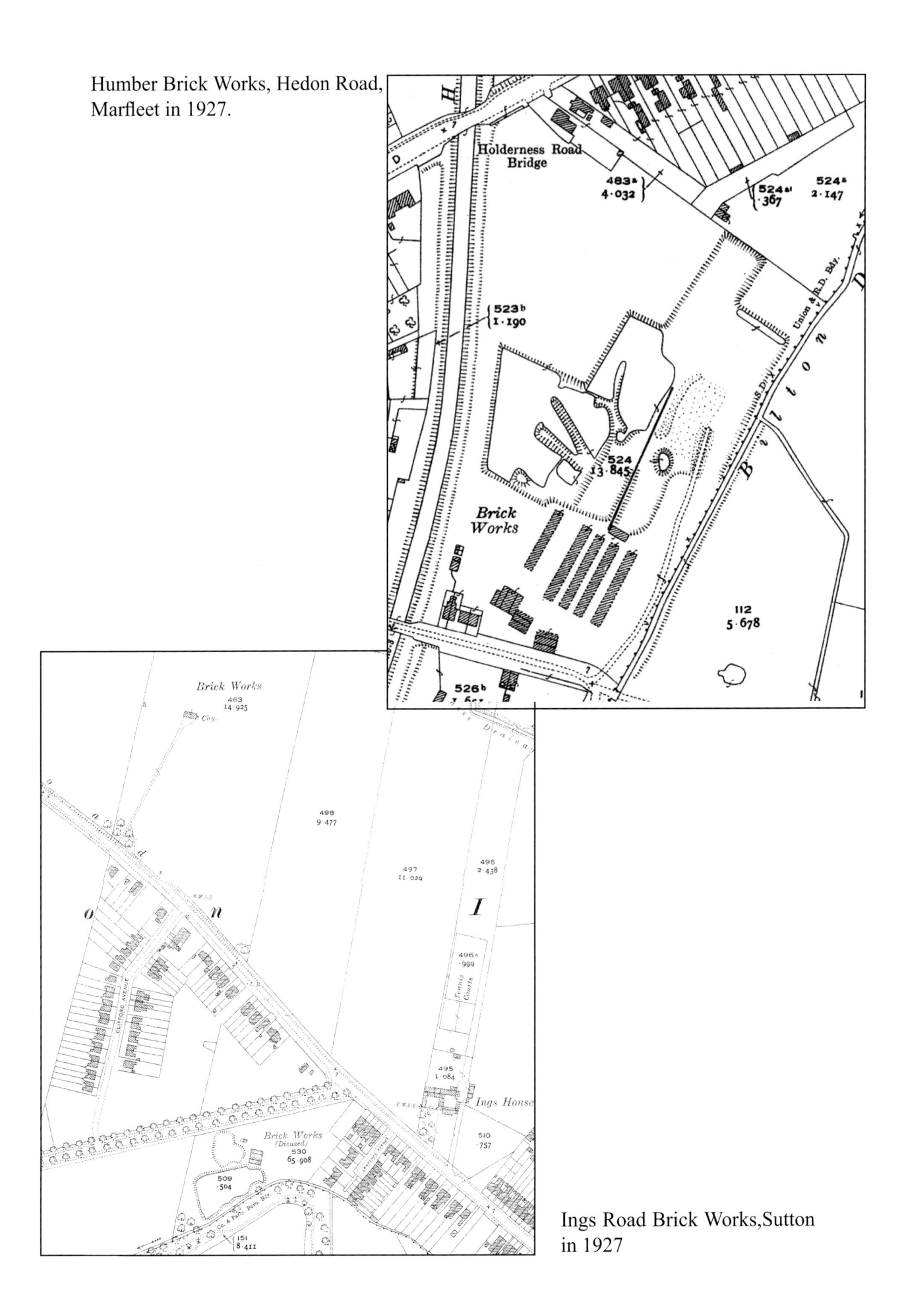

Ings Road Brick Works, Sutton in 1927

Chapter 19

FRIENDLY SOCIETIES INCLUDING ODDFELLOWS

Many of the brickmakers and other craftsmen mentioned in this book (bricklayers, builders, carpenters, etc.,) were members of Friendly Societies. The majority from Castle and Sible Hedingham were members of the Loyal Webster Lodge of Oddfellows, based in Sible Hedingham, which was affiliated to the Manchester Unity of Oddfellows. The three brothers, Harry, John and Fred Corder joined the Lodge on 7th October 1905. It is known that William, Walter, Bert and Percy Corder were also members as were Percy and George Boreham and William Willett.

The Loyal Webster Lodge was originally a Sick Benefit Club carried on by the Misses Eleanor and Elizabeth Amelia Webster of The Bays, Swan Street, Sible Hedingham. (1) It was called the 'Hedingham Working Men's Club' and was established in 1889 with Herbert G. Benson, an Auctioneer's Clerk of Pye Corner, Castle Hedingham as Secretary, Robert Lewis Webb Assistant Secretary and Dr. Henry Joseph Twamley Treasurer. The Chairman was Mark Gentry, a Sible Hedingham master brickmaker and at the first annual dinner held in January 1890 he was elected as President. (2) In 1902 the former club joined the Independent Order of Oddfellows and became one of many lodges included in the Colchester and Maldon District, which was founded in 1845. (3) The Misses Webster were great benefactors to Sible Hedingham and in particular to the welfare of its residents. In 1884 they built six almshouses in memory of their Mother and in 1912 and 1914 provided new bells for the Church. No philanthropic work was undertaken without their assistance and they never spared themselves or their money when the welfare of residents was under consideration. (4)

The Lodge meetings were held in the Assembly Rooms, Swan Street, owned by Mark Gentry. (5) The Lodge Secretary for many years was Robert L. Webb (1873-1945) who was employed in the office of Mark Gentry and actually lived next door to George Corder in Wethersfield Road. When Robert Webb retired as Secretary through ill health in 1939 the Webster Lodge was one of the largest in the Colchester and Maldon District with between 800 and 900 members. The Lodge Master was Eli Cornish, C.C., J.P., another Sible Hedingham master brickmaker. The Colchester and Maldon District Meeting was held in Sible Hedingham in 1907 and the Webster Lodge provided the following Provincial Grand Masters for the Colchester and Maldon District:

1914 Frederick George Bishop, miller, corn merchant, agricultural and electrical engineer and Chairman of Sible Hedingham Parish Council.

1926 William Wright Raynham, D.C.M., a soldier who took part in the South African and Egyptian campaigns. In circa 1905 he was employed by Mark Gentry as a foreman at his Highfield Brick Works. William Raynham was also a baker on his own account and one of the earliest members of the Lodge. In the First World War he rejoined the army serving in the Northumberland Fusiliers in which he was given a commission in December 1915. After the war he was employed by Rippers Limited.

1941 C. Westrop.

By 1947 the Webster Lodge had 520 adult and 136 junior members and assets worth £11,754. (7) A long serving secretary was (Sister) Mrs. Maud Smith, who in her young days had been a suffragette and eventually lived until she was over a hundred.

Prior to the First World War regular Friendly Society Parades were held in Sible Hedingham organised by Eli Cornish, Harry Corder, Alfred Metson (farmer), Ernest Savill Willis (coachbuilder and Clerk to Sible Hedingham Parish Council) and others. The parades assembled in Webster's Meadow next to Bay Cottage, Swan Street. After the First World War the parades met in the Assembly Rooms. The Webster Lodge, including many brickmakers and the Hedinghams Brass Band, of which Bert and his brother Ted Corder were members, took prominent positions. The Friendly Societies and Band paraded to different local churches each year including St. Peter's, Sible Hedingham, St. Nicholas and the Congregational Chapel (now URC), Castle Hedingham. The members of the Webster Lodge who took part wore their regalia including a collarette. Each Friendly Society had a banner and the parades were well attended and impressive. (8)

The Oddfellows thrived until well into the twentieth century and even after the introduction of the state pension and the National Health Service. (9) The majority of brickmakers in the Hedinghams were Oddfellows who received financial benefits in the event of illness, injury or unemployment as well as assistance with burial fees. Even in recent years the families of former members of the Webster Lodge received financial contributions towards the cost of funerals.

A few Sible Hedingham brickmakers were members of the Loyal Courtauld Lodge of Oddfellows in Halstead. In Gestingthorpe, many brickmakers and potters were members of The Rayner Friendly Society, formed by the Rayner family of master brickmakers. It did good work in the parish from its formation in 1863, until it was taken over by the Manchester Unity of Oddfellows on 4th November 1912, following a meeting of the Lodge held in Gestingthorpe Schoolroom. (10) The brickmakers in Gestingthorpe continued to receive similar benefits from the Lodge to those enjoyed by the former Friendly Society. This support was very useful to brickmakers and their families particularly before the arrival of the generous benefits enjoyed today.

A Friendly Societies Parade in Church Street, Sible Hedingham.

A Friendly Societies Parade in Church Street approaching Sible Hedingham Church.

The Hedinghams Brass Band in St. James' Street, Castle Hedingham left to right: Ted Corder, with his brother Bert Corder standing behind, Tom Parsons (with trombone), Ernest Chatten (double bass), Lewis Wiseman (conductor in plain clothes with cap) and Arnold Howard the small boy in front of him.

Certificates of Harry and Fred Corder as members of the Loyal Webster Lodge of Oddlfellows.

Chapter 20

RAYMOND JOHN CORDER, BRICKMAKER AND
ADRIAN CORDER-BIRCH, MEMBER OF BRITISH BRICK SOCIETY

Raymond John Corder

After some one hundred and seventy years, two members of the Corder family were still actively involved in completely different capacities in the brickmaking industry at the beginning of this millennium.

Raymond John Corder, born 19th November 1966, was employed as a brickmaker by Bulmer Brick and Tile Co. Limited of Hole Farm, Bulmer since the 1980s. (1) He is descended from William and Frances Corder (formerly Frances Warren) (see chapter 1) through both their eldest son William (1767-1844) and their fourth son Joseph (1777-1869). William's granddaughter, Charlotte Eliza Corder (1839-1924) married Joseph's grandson, Charles Corder (1837-1877) in 1858. (2) Raymond is their great, great, great grandson and is a member of the seventh generation of the Corder family to be involved in the brickmaking industry.

On 6th February 2006 he appeared on BBC2 television at Bulmer Brick Works, making bricks for renovation work at Hampton Court Palace. At Bulmer all bricks are still made by hand in the traditional method; they are dried in hacks and drying sheds and fired in down-draught kilns. Raymond became an experienced hand-made brickmaker, specialising in ornamental bricks; the results of his craft can be seen in the restoration work of many important buildings in the country apart from Hampton Court Palace. Unfortunately Raymond was forced to retire as a brickmaker in 2008 as a result of back trouble and is now self employed in a different trade. (3)

Raymond Corder making bricks at Bulmer Brick and Tile Works. Left to right: (1) Throwing a warp of clay into a brick mould, (2) removing the surplus clay from the top of the mould and (3) the completed 'green' brick still in its mould. (Photographs courtesy of Peter Minter).

Adrian Corder-Birch

Adrian Corder-Birch has been a member of the British Brick Society since 1978 and its Hon. Auditor since 1989. He has also been a member of the British Archaeological Association and its Brick Section since 1978. He is interested in many aspects of industrial archaeology and in particular the clay industries. He has assisted the Historic Environment Branch of Essex County Council with the compilation of a number of comparative surveys of industrial sites and monuments. These have included industrial housing in Essex, which includes housing associated with extractive industries such as brick and tile manufacturing.

He is often consulted regarding the history of the brickmaking industry and the sites of former brickworks. In Essex he has advised the Essex County Council Field Archaeology Unit upon archaeological excavations of former brickworks at Colchester (in association with Colchester Archaeological Trust), Chelmsford, Sible Hedingham, Parkeston, Wendons Ambo and various other locations where he has identified and interpreted remains.

Archaeological excavation by Essex County Council Field Archaeology Unit at the former Langthorne Brick Works, Wethersfield Road, Sible Hedingham during January and February 2006. This view, photographed by the author, shows part of an engine house in the northern part of the site. The excavation was necessary in advance of the construction of lagoon 2 of a flood alleviation scheme.

Adrian has also assisted English Heritage with identifying significant remains, sites of long duration and other important features for inclusion in its clay industries monuments protection programme (MPP). Three locations mentioned in this book have been included in the English Heritage shortlist (which is confidential); this illustrates the importance of the research, site visits and recording undertaken by him over the years. Some sites have warranted statutory protection either through listing or scheduling, which provides a sound framework for managing and protecting the resource through the planning process.

In particular he has encouraged archaeologists and others, with both Essex County Council and English Heritage, to record 'brick marks' where found on bricks from all types of buildings, principally in Essex. These brick marks have frequently assisted with identifying in which brickworks the bricks for a particular building were made.

Adrian Corder-Birch continues the Corder family tradition of its close association with the brickmaking industry through researching and recording the history of former brick, tile and pottery works, principally in Essex, for future publications and the protection of appropriate sites.

An historic moment: the author making his first brick, being the fifth generation of the Corder family to do so. This event took place at the Michelmersh Brick Works, Hampshire on 16th May 1992. The photograph was taken by Michael Hammett, Dip.Arch., A.R.I.B.A., then the Hon. Secretary of the British Brick Society and Senior Architect in the Professional Services Department of the Brick Development Association.

A selection of brickmaking tools. Left to right: Two top-spades used to dig out clay (which could also be used for cutting drains). A Cuckle (or Cockle) an implement used to place pug on the brickmaker's table (note the cuckle is upside down and its wooden handle is missing). Brickmakers or clay spade, often called a graft, used to dig out clay during the winter months.

GLOSSARY

This is a glossary of brickmaking terms used in this book only and not a complete glossary. Some terms vary from area to area and even from village to village as the author has noticed different terms used between Sible Hedingham and Bulmer.

Bearing off barrow	Also called an off bearing barrow and a cradle barrow; used for carrying green bricks to the hacks or drying sheds. These barrows had special springs to minimise vibration and held about 30 'green' bricks.
Bow	A bow with wire between its ends used to remove the surplus clay from the top of the mould. A strike was also used for the same purpose - see below.
Bullnose	A brick with a rounded header (the short end).
Chalk	Used with clay to form white or yellow bricks - see Suffolk bricks below.
Clamp	A temporary kiln formed by setting dried bricks together in a special manner without a permanent kiln.
Cradle barrow	See bearing off barrow above.
Crowding barrow	Also known as a kiln barrow - used for taking dried bricks to the kiln and later for unloading the kiln.
Cuckle (or Cockle)	An implement used to place pug on the brickmaker's table, designed with a narrow curved blade to prevent pug sticking to it.
Down-draught kiln	Usually circular or 'beehive' shaped, although some were rectangular. They had several furnaces around the outside. The heat rose to the centre and was drawn out through the bottom of the kiln along a tunnel and through a chimney. The bricks were fired with the heat being drawn in a downwards direction hence a 'down-draught' kiln.
Drying sheds	Large sheds, usually wooden and often heated, in which to dry 'green' products including bricks, tiles, pipes and pottery.
Frog	The indentation in the bedding surface of a brick, which often includes the maker's name. It reduces the brick's weight and provides a key for mortar.
Ganger	Foreman of gang of workmen

Green brick	A freshly made brick, prior to firing.
Hack	Derived from 'hack stead' a drying place for 'green' bricks.
Hack ground	Area containing hacks - rows of open sided hack covers for drying bricks.
Kiln	Permanent brick structures used for firing bricks - see down-draught and up-draught kilns.
Kiln barrow	See crowding barrow above.
Loo (or lew) boards	Were used for protecting 'green' products in the hacks from drying too rapidly through sun, draught or rain. The wooden frames were covered with hessian sacks or matting to allow the free circulation of air; the frames stood against, or hung from, the hack covers.
Mould	Frame of wood or metal without top or bottom.
Pallet board	Thin board used to handle 'green' bricks before being taken for drying.
Pamments (or pammets)	Large square floor or paving bricks (paviors); special hard burnt bricks.
Pug	Prepared clay in a plastic state ready for use by brickmakers.
Pugging	Preparation of clay by kneading and working ready for use.
Pug-Mill	Large metal cylinder containing a central shaft with blades attached which when revolved mixes the clay to a uniform plastic state. Sand and water is added as appropriate and the resulting 'pug' is ready for use by the brickmaker. Originally powered by horses and later by machine.
Red products	Many shades of reds are obtained due to the quantity of iron oxide in the clay.
Skintling	Turning the bricks at a diagonal angle as they are drying so that the sun and wind can dry all surfaces.
Squints	Special moulded bricks which have a corner removed for decorative purposes.
Stock board	Fixed to brickmaker's table upon which the mould is placed and held in position whilst bricks are made.

Strike	A piece of wood or metal pulled across the top of a mould to remove the surplus clay. A bow with wire was also used for the same purpose (see Bow above).
Suffolk bricks	Should be made exclusively in Suffolk but the term is often applied to white or very pale yellow bricks made in adjoining counties using a mixture of chalk and clay.
Up-draught kiln	Square or rectangular in shape and had two chambers one above the other. The fire was in the lower chamber which contained two to five fire holes or tunnels and the bricks were fired in the upper chamber hence the term 'up-draught' meaning the bricks were fired with the heat rising. These kilns had one doorway in the upper chamber to load and unload and an open top. When loaded the doorway was filled up with a few courses of old bricks which were temporarily filled with clay paste. The top was covered with layers of old bricks to protect the dried bricks below. The burners opened and closed the gaps between these old bricks to control the draught, this was known as platting.
Wash-Mill	A circular brick tank about 14 foot in diameter and 4 foot 6 inches deep, with a central pillar, which acts as a pivot on which is hung a horizontal frame containing a number of suspended harrows. The frame is rotated by horse or machine and water is added to the clay to wash it and form a slurry, which runs out to settling tanks or wash backs. This process separates stones from the clay.
White bricks	See Suffolk bricks above.

Peter Minter with finished products at Bulmer Brick and Tile Works where bricks continue to be made by hand in the traditional method. In the background are rows of hacks where 'green' bricks are drying.

BIBLIOGRAPHY, SOURCES, NOTES AND REFERENCES

Author's Preface

1. Essex Countryside, December 1968, Vol. 17 No. 143, pages 36 & 37

2. East Anglian Magazine, January 1972, pages 120 to 122
   The Halstead and District Local History Society, newsletter March 1979, Vol. 3 No. 7, pages 4 to 6
   British Brick Society, Information No. 36, May 1985, pages 15 to 17
   Essex Journal, Winter 1985, Vol. 20 No. 3, pages 66 & 67
   Colne Valley Newslines, No. 1, 1985 and No. 5, 1986
   Essex 'full of profitable thinges', 1996, pages 433 to 450

A brief introduction to the craft of brickmaking by hand

1. Essex 'full of profitable thinges' 1996 page 439

Chapter 1   John Corder (1806-1880) and his early years in Gestingthorpe

1. Marriage, Baptism & Burial Registers for Gestingthorpe Church: ERO., D/P 85

2. Marriage Licence: ERO., D/ALL 1800

3. Baptism Register for Gestingthorpe Church: ERO., D/P 85

4. Marriage Register for Belchamp Walter Church: ERO., D/P 215/1/6

5. Baptism Register for Gestingthorpe Church: ERO., D/P 85

6. Census Return 1841: HO 107/332/1

7. Overhall Court Roll 1562

8. The Downs Family and Iron Foundry at Gestingthorpe, by Adrian Corder-Birch, Essex Journal, Spring 2005 pages 22 to 26

9. Map of Gestingthorpe by Isaac Johnson of Sudbury 1804: ERO., D/P 85/3

10. Tithe Map of Gestingthorpe 1838: ERO., D/CT 149

11. The Gestingthorpe Pot Works, by Alfred Hills, M.A., 1944

12 Castle Hedingham Pottery (1837-1905), by R. J. Bradley, 1968

Chapter 2   John Corder (1806-1880) at Castle and Sible Hedingham

1. Census Return 1851: HO 107/1784

2. The definition of a journeyman was one who worked away from home, who had completed an apprenticeship but had not set up as a master himself. It is therefore possible that John was employed by other master brickmakers elsewhere but no evidence of this has been found

3. The Downs Family and Iron Foundry at Gestingthorpe, by Adrian Corder-Birch, Essex Journal, Spring 2005 pages 22 to 26

4. Census Return 1851: HO 107/1788

5. John and Thomas Eley were corn millers at Tower Mill and maltsters and farmers at Wash Farm, Sible Hedingham.

6. An Act for granting to His Majesty certain Rates and Duties upon Bricks and Tiles made in Great Britain; and for laying additional Duties in Bricks and Tiles imported into the same 1784, as amended in 1785.

7. An Act for granting to His Majesty certain additional Duties on Bricks and Tiles made in or imported into Great Britain 1794.

8. An Act to repeal the Duties of Excise payable in Great Britain and to grant other Duties in lieu thereof, as grants any Duty or Drawbacks on Bricks 1803.

9. An Act for repealing the Duties and Drawbacks of Excise on Tiles 1833.

10. An Act to repeal the Duties and Drawbacks of Excise on Bricks 1850.

11. Census Return 1861: RG 9/1112

12. Census Return 1871: RG10/1699

13. Section 5 and the First Schedule of An Act to amend the Acts relating to Factories and Workshops 1871 and cited as "The Factory and Workshop Act 1871".

14. Post Office Directories of Essex 1874, 1876 and 1878

15. Death certificate and burial register of Castle Hedingham Independent Meeting Chapel

16. Edward Bingham (1829-1916) was an ornamental potter in Castle Hedingham until 1906 having succeeded his father, Edward Abel Bingham (1799-1872) who had commenced making pottery in Castle Hedingham in 1837

Chapter 3 **William Corder (1835-1903) and Southey Green Brick, Tile and Pottery Works, Sible Hedingham**

1. Census Return 1851: HO 107/1784

2. Sible Hedingham Land Tax Assessments 1833-1865 and 1866-1922, ERO., D/Z 2/7/25C and D/Z 2/18/24

3. The Place Names of Essex, by P. H. Reaney, Cambridge University Press, 1969 page 443

4. Ibid

5. Essex Archaeological News, Winter 1972 pages 7 and 8 Essex Archaeology and History, Vol. 8, 1976 page 268 The Sible Hedingham medieval kilns and their pottery is the subject of a forthcoming comprehensive publication by the Essex Field Archaeology Unit

6. The Place Names of Essex, by P. H. Reaney, Cambridge University Press, 1969 page 443

7. A map dated 1717 in the archives of Hedingham Castle, courtesy of Jason Lindsay, indicates that Southey Green may be a corruption of South Green, which was the southern point of the Hedingham Castle Estate during the eighteenth century. (It is known that North End, Little Yeldham was the northern point of the estate).

8. The Court Books of the Manor of Prayors, Sible Hedingham (4 vols. 1733-1935), ERO., D/Dsm. M 17-20

9. Sale catalogue, 1864, ERO., D/F 6/1/17

10. Census Return 1861: RG9/1112

11. Census Return 1871: RG10/1699

12. Census Return 1881: RG11/1804

13. Sible Hedingham Land Tax Assessments 1866-1922, ERO., D/Z 2/18/24. John Savill was principally an auctioneer, land surveyor, estate and insurance agent of Swan Street, Sible Hedingham but later became a landowner and farmer at Orange Hall, Gosfield.

14. Census Return 1881: RG11/1804

15. Sale particulars of Warrens Farm, ERO., D/DBmT109 and B.2570

16. Census Return 1881: RG11/1804

17. Sale particulars of Hedingham Castle Estate, ERO., sale cat. A 1071

18. John Cutts (1797-1882) who was born at Stebbing became an attorney, solicitor, commissioner for oaths, landowner and farmer and lived at Little B a r d f i e l d Hall. In 1861 he farmed 800 acres and employed 40 men and 8 boys. He was Lord of the Manor of Little Bardfield and a manor called Fitzralphs which extended into Thaxted. His improvements to Little Bardfield Hall and Farm included the erection of some ornamental and commodious cottages. He died on 21st July 1882 at his home aged 85 years. His will was later proved by Sophia Cutts, his widow.

19. Sale particulars, ERO., D/F 35/7/575

20. Sible Hedingham Tithe Map D/CT 174

21. Ibid

22. Halstead Gazette, 19th June 1890

23. The Court Books of the Manor of Prayors, Sible Hedingham (4 vols. 1733-1935), ERO., D/Dsm. M 17-20

24. Deeds of the Brickyard including the two houses and those of Warrens Farm

25. The British Clayworker, July 1895 p. 102
    Halstead Gazettes of 13th June 1895 and 16th January 1896
    The Weekly Notes, 8th June 1895 pages 260 & 261 & 15th June 1895 page 292

26. Minute Book of Assessment Committee of Halstead Union, 1896

27. Information courtesy of William Martin

28. Halstead Gazette, 3rd August 1899

29. Death Certificate and Burial Register of Castle Hedingham Chapel

Chapter 4 Harry Corder (1873-1942) and Southey Green Brick, Tile and Pottery Works

1. Directory in The Brick and Pottery Trades Journal, May 1905 page 194

2. Chimney Pots and Stacks, by Valentine Fletcher, Centaur Press Limited, 1968

3. Land Value Duty Survey 1910: ERO., A/R 2/2/18

4. Commonwealth War Graves Commission records

5. Halstead Gazette, 23rd May 1924

6. Invoice, 9th August 1918

7. Halstead Gazette, 8th April 1921

8. Invoice December 1928

9. Account books of Harry Rippingale (1889-1978) in the author's possession

10. Census Return 1911: Sible Hedingham Schedule No: 213

11. Halstead Gazette, 6th March 1942

12. Loo boards (or lew boards) -see glossary

13. The Discovery of Britain - A Guide to Archaeology, by Jack Lindsay, The Merlin Press Limited, 1958 pages 148 to 149

Chapter 5   John Corder (1876-1922)

1. Census Return 1891: RG12/1420

2. Census Return 1901: RG13/1721

3. Census Return 1911: Sible Hedingham Schedule No. 202

4. Halstead Gazette 21st July 1922

Chapter 6   Fred Corder (1885-1961)

1. Census Return 1901: RG13/1721

2. Census Return 1911: Sible Hedingham Schedule No. 202

3. Halstead Gazette, 12th October 1917

Chapter 7   Potter's Hall Brick, Tile and Pottery Works, Great Yeldham

1. Post Office and Kelly's Directories of Essex from 1874 to 1908

2. OS 25 in. Maps of 1876 and 1897

3. A History of Great Yeldham, by Adrian Corder-Birch, Halstead and District Local History Society, 1994

4. Sale Catalogue: ERO., B2682

Chapter 8   Park Hall Road Brick Works, Gosfield

1.   OS 25in. Map of 1897

2.   John Johnson 1732-1814 Georgian Architect and County Surveyor of Essex, by Nancy Briggs, Essex Record Office, 1991 pages 113 & 114

Chapter 9   George Corder (1863-1938) and his sons William Dan Corder (1886-1970), Herbert Charles Corder (1888-1970) and Walter Edward Corder (1896-1983)

1.   Census Return 1881 RG11/1804

2.   Census Return 1891 RG12/1419

3.   Census Return 1901 RG13/1721

4.   The Brickbuilder, April 1898 pages ii to iv
     The British Clayworker, April 1908 page 11

5.   The original indenture dated 1st September 1902 and endorsed 16th June 1906 is in the possession of the author

6.   Bessie Turner died 22nd November 1918 at The Bays, Sible Hedingham, the home of Eleanor and Elizabeth Amelia Webster (see chapter 19)

7.   Census Return 1881 RG11/1825

8.   Halstead Gazette 12th June 1931

9.   The British Army World War One Service Records at the National Archives ref: WO 363

10. Frank Redgewell Twitchett (1867-1942) farmed Clare Downs and Cut Bush Farms at Belchamp St. Paul and Priory Farm at Clare. He was manager of Lloyds Bank at Clare, Clerk and later Chairman of Clare Parish Council. His mother Mary Twitchett nee Redgewell (1829-1910) was the elder sister of Hannah Redgewell (1831-1867), the first wife of William Corder (1835-1903), the grandparents of Walter Corder

Chapter 10   Brick Kiln Hill Brick Works, Castle Hedingham, Robert Corder (1833-1915) and family

1.   Account book of George Hardy & Son; ERO., D/DU 447/9

2.   Halstead Gazette 27th May 1897

3.   Land Value Duty Survey 1910: ERO., A/R 2/2/18 and A/R 1/1/52

4.   Halstead Gazette 12th November 1915

5.   Census Return 1871: RG10/1699

6.   Castle Hedingham Pottery (1837-1905) by R. J. Bradley, reprinted from The Connoisseur, February, March and April 1968

7.   The Discovery of Britain - A Guide to Archaeology, by Jack Lindsay, The Merlin Press Limited, 1958 pages 189 to 191 and 228 to 229

8.   Ibid. page 194

Chapter 11   John Corder (1863-1957), Edward John Corder (1886-1938), Bert William Corder (1889-1955) and Percy James Corder (1896-1989)

1   Census Return 1901: RG13/1721

2.   Census Return 1911: Thundersley Schedule No: 171

3.   Memorandum and Articles of Association of The Sible Hedingham Red Brick Company Limited dated 22nd December 1919

4.   Census Return 1901: RG13/1721

5.   Census Return 1911: Thundersley Schedule No: 171

6.   Halstead Gazette 21st January 1955

7.   ERO., D/Du 1018/18

8.   ERO., D/RH Pb 1/81

9.   Census Return 1911: Sible Hedingham Schedule No: 135

10.   A Pictorial History of Sible Hedingham, by Adrian Corder-Birch, Halstead and District Local History Society, 1988 and second edition, 1996

Chapter 12   Edward Corder (1868-1940) and the Manor Brick Works, Thundersley

1.   Recollections of an old Woodpecker, by H. T. Ripper, 1947 page 28
     Halstead Gazette, 16th June 1916

2.   Census Return 1901: RG13/1721

3. ERO., D/UBe 2/1/1074

4. ERO., D/UBe 2/1/4323

5. Census Return 1911: Thundersley Schedule No. 171

6. The British Clayworker, September 1905 page 200

7. The Brick and Pottery Trades Journal, 1st February 1910 page 92
   The Brickbuilder, February 1910 pages xviii and lxxxiv
   The Brick and Pottery Trades Journal, 1st May 1910 page 240

8. Census Return 1911: Thundersley Schedule No: 172

9. Recollections of an old Woodpecker, by H. T. Ripper, 1947 pages 114 and 115

10. Some of the information for this chapter was provided by Gayle Thomson nee Corder, Captain Edward (Jim) Corder, Donald Corder, Douglas Corder and their late father Edward D. Corder.

Chapter 13 David Corder (1837-1881), James Corder (1840-1907) and Alfred Corder (1845-1898)

1. Census Return 1851: HO107/1784

2. Marriage Certificate

3. Death Certificates

4. Census Return 1851: HO107/1784

5. Marriage Certificate

6. Recollections of an old Woodpecker, by H. T. Ripper, 1947 p. 28

7. Hunt for Machinery - The Rise, Success and Demise of R. Hunt & Co. Limited of Earls Colne 1825-1988 by P. J. Burton-Hopkins, Halstead and District Local History Society, 1995, pages 18 & 19

8. Halstead Gazette, 7th September 1907

9. Census Return 1861: RG9/1112

10. Halstead Times, 10th June 1865

11. Halstead Gazette, 26th November 1898

12. Marriage Certificate

13. Marriage Certificate

14. Essex Directories 1848 to 1926

Chapter 14   Henry Corder (1850-1934)

1. Census Return 1861: RG9/1112

2. Census Return 1871: RG10/1699

3. Census Return 1881: RG11/1804

4. Census Return 1891: RG12/1420

5. Census Return 1901: RG13/1719

6. Birth Certificate

7. Kelly's Directories of Essex from 1902 to 1933

8. Census Return 1911: Halstead schedule no: 135

9. The majority of information for this chapter was provided by the late Alfred Cecil Corder (1901-1990) the only son of Henry Corder

Chapter 15   Related brickmaking family from Castle Hedingham: Samuel Westrop (1830-1867) and Alfred Westrop (1853-1879)

1. Census Return 1861: RG9/1112

2. Census Return 1871: RG10/1699

3. Death Certificate

Chapter 16   Related brickmaking families from Sible Hedingham: The Boreham, Brett, King, Gepp and Willett families and William James Wiseman (1882-1959)

1. Marriage Certificate

2. Halstead Gazette, 18th May 1917

3. Commonwealth War Graves Commission records.

4. Census Return 1911: Sible Hedingham schedule no: 140

5. Halstead Gazette, 16th June 1910

6. Halstead Gazette, 25th May 1913

7. Census Return 1901: RG13/1721

8. Ibid

9. Census Return 1911: Sible Hedingham Schedule No: 78

10. Halstead Gazette, 2nd January 1931

11. Census Return 1901: RG13/1721

12. Ibid

13. Census Return 1911: Sible Hedingham Schedule No: 67

14. Halstead Gazette, 8th May 1959

Chapter 17   Related brickmaking families from Gestingthorpe: The Finch, Felton and Rippingale families and Harry Rippingale (1889-1978)

1. Death Certificate

2. Census Return 1911: Gestingthorpe Schedule No: 19

3. Commonwealth War Graves Commission records

4. The author is grateful to Ashley Cooper for permission to reprint the quotes and for some of the information in this chapter about the Finch family of Gestingthorpe and their association with the brick and tile making industry. Ashley interviewed and recorded their recollections in his excellent series of books, published by Bulmer Historical Society including:
The Long Furrow 1982 Heart of Our History 1994 Our Mother Earth 1998

5. Halstead Gazette, 21st August 1931

6. Information courtesy of the late Lily Rippingale, nee Corder (1896-1983)

7. Census Return 1911: Gestingthorpe Schedule No: 18

8. Halstead Gazette, 16th October 1917

9. The Gestingthorpe Pot Works, by Alfred Hills, M.A., (Reprinted from the Essex Review, Vol. LIII, pp 37-45, April 1944)

10. Essex Directories 1832 and 1839

11. Census Return 1841: HO107/325

12. Census Return 1851: HO107/

13. Census Return 1861: RG9/1079

14. Bulmer Then and Now by W.E.A. 1979 and ERO., SA 17/790/1

15. Marriage Certificate. During the 1970's the author asked Harry and Lily Rippingale why they had married on Christmas Day. They explained that Harry worked every day of the year including the morning of Christmas Day and as the afternoon of Christmas Day was his half day holiday a year that was the only time he had spare to get married. The same had applied to other Corder ancestors during the nineteenth century.

16. Sound Archive at ERO., ref: SA 17/790/1; a taped interview of Harry Rippingale by Basil Slaughter made 1974. The author who had many conversations with Harry Rippingale before his death in 1978, listened to the recording in 2009. It was poignant to hear his voice again over thirty years later.

17. A History of Public Transport in the Halstead Area, by Eric Axten, Halstead and District Local History Society, 1980. Further reading: The Country Bus, by John Hibbs, David and Charles, 1986 and Heart of our History, by Ashley Cooper, Bulmer Historical Society, 1994.

18. Halstead Gazette, 17th February 1956

19. Census Return 1911: Gestingthorpe Schedule No. 123

Chapter 18   Finch Brick Works at Hull, Yorkshire

1. Census Return 1851: HO107/2362

2. Census Return 1861: RG9/3589

3. Census Return 1871: RG10/4784

4. Directories of Kingston upon Hull 1872 to 1892

5. Will and four Codicils of George Finch - probate granted 2nd July 1892.

6. Directories of Kingston upon Hull 1892 to 1895

7. The British Clayworker, June 1938 page 103

8. The Directory of British Clayworkers, 1938 page 127

9. Memories of the Village of Marfleet mainly 1920's and 1930's, by Geoffrey Edwards, 2001

10. East Riding Archives and Local Studies ref: CCHU/2/4/8/4/44

11. Kelly's Directory of Merchants, Manufacturers and Shippers, 1946

12. East Riding Archives and Local Studies ref: CCER/2/8/1/65

13. Information courtesy of Ann Los

Chapter 19   Friendly Societies including Oddfellows

1. A Pictorial History of Sible Hedingham, by Adrian Corder-Birch, Halstead and District Local History Society, 1988 and second edition, 1996

2. Halstead Gazette, 16th January 1890

3. Oddfellows in Essex, Centenary 1945, A short history of the Colchester and Maldon District, by John S. Appleby, 1947

4. A Pictorial History of Sible Hedingham, by Adrian Corder-Birch, Halstead and District Local History Society, 1988 and second edition, 1996

5. The former Assembly Rooms (sometimes called the Oddfellows Hall) was situated at the rear of 33 Swan Street. The building was previously an iron foundry purchased by Mark Gentry in 1892, which he converted into a Public Hall and Constitutional Club. The building was sold and demolished in 1950. The first caretaker was George Walter Harrington, a baker, who lived nearby. He was succeeded by William Willett (1833-1913) an old soldier with over twenty years service who had fought in the Crimean and Malay wars. He had a military funeral and was an uncle to Alice Ann Corder (nee Willett).

6. Halstead Gazette, 16th June 1939

7. Oddfellows in Essex, Centenary 1945, A short history of the Colchester and Maldon District, by John S. Appleby, 1947

8. A Pictorial History of Sible Hedingham, by Adrian Corder-Birch, Halstead and District Local History Society, 1988 and second edition, 1996

9. Discovering Friendly and Fraternal Societies: Their Badges and Regalia, by Victoria Solt Dennis, Shire Publications Limited, 2005

10. Gestingthorpe Parish Magazine, November 1912

Chapter 20   Raymond John Corder and Adrian Corder-Birch

1. There are eight photographs of Raymond Corder making bricks at Bulmer Brick Works in the book, BRICK A World History, by James W. P. Campbell, Thames and Hudson Limited, 2003. The photographs, taken by Will Pryce, appear on pages 163, 174 and 175. Dr. James Campbell is a Fellow in Architecture and History of Art, a Director of Conservation with Finch Forman Architects and a former Chairman of the British Brick Society

2. Following the death of Charles Corder, his widow married William Ives (1836-1905) whose younger sister, Mary Ann Ives (1841-1874) married Ezekiel Thomas Corder (1842-1897) in 1863. (see chapter 17)

3. Information courtesy of Peter and Tony Minter of Bulmer Brick and Tile Company Limited

Glossary

1. Modern Brickmaking, by Alfred B. Searle, Third Edition, Ernest Benn Limited, 1931 and information kindly supplied by Peter Minter

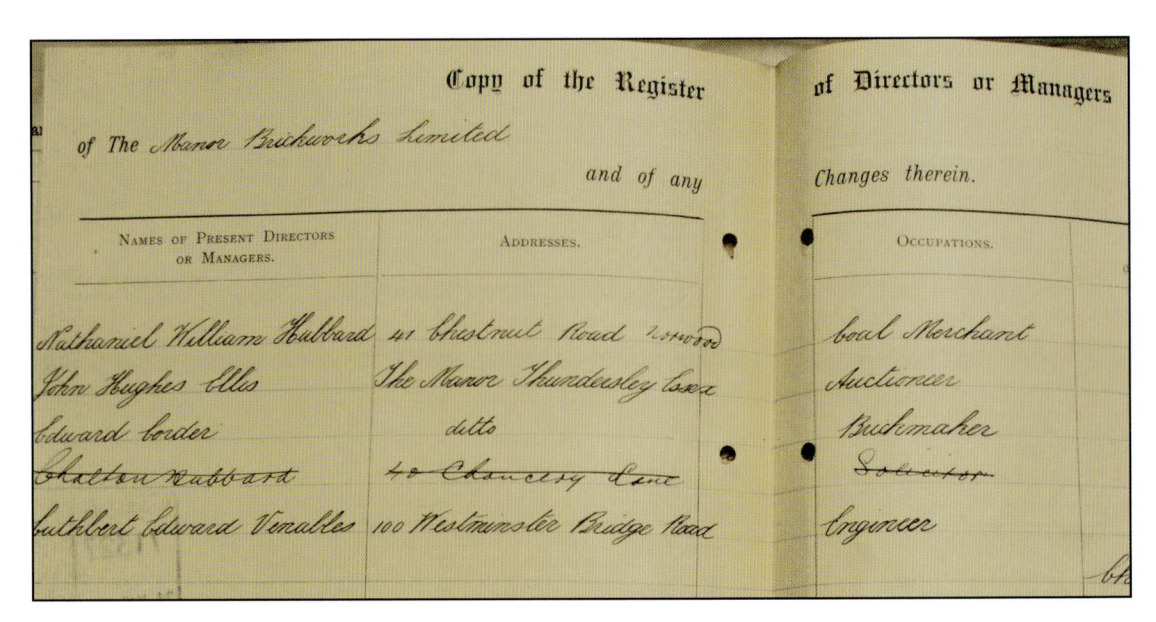

An extract from the Register of Directors or Managers of The Manor Brickworks Limited, including Edward Corder, Brickmaker. This document, dated 24th August 1907, is from the company file held at the National Archive Office and was kindly sent to the author by Robin Waywell.

INDEX

A

Allen, Gertrude, 107
Alphamstone, 99
Atkinson, His Honour Judge Tindal, 121

B

Baines, Mrs. Lana, 24
Balls & Balls, 47
Balls, James Mayhew, 118
Balls, Robert, 83
Bareham, Percy Ralph, 102
Barton & Co., 49,50
Beavis, Joanne & Richard, 67
Belchamp Rural District Council, 99
Belchamp St. Paul, 81,99
Belchamp Walter, 13
Benson, Herbert G., 139
Bingham, Edward, 15,21,24,38,87-90,105,118
Bingham, Edward Abel, 15
Bingham, Edward William & Hephzibah, 88
Bingham family, 15,87,88
Bingham, Richard James, 87,105,112
Bishop, (Frederick) George, 25,139
Bishop's Stortford, 45
Blackie, Dr. Margery, 81
Bocking, Benjamin, 44
Bocking, Charles, 32,66,100
Bocking, Robert, 44,45
Boorer, Lewis, 100
Boorer, Martha, 88
Boreham, Charles Humphrey, 119,120
Boreham, Dollar Signor, 119
Boreham, Evelyn Gladys, 119
Boreham family, 119
Boreham, George Oliver, 119,139
Boreham, Henry Joseph, 119
Boreham, Isaac & Louisa, 119
Boreham, James Vero, 119
Boreham, Percy, 119,139
Boreham, William, 30
Bradley, R. J., 87
Bradridge, T. & Co., 92
Bragg, Harold, 44
Brett, Alice Agnes, 94,98,120,121
Brett, Eliza, 120
Brett, Elizabeth, 121
Brett family, 120
Brett, Herb, 103
Brett, John, senior and junior, 120
Brett, Robert, 120
Brick Development Association, 145
Brick Kiln Hill Brick Works, 83-86,94,105, 111-113,117,118

British Archaeological Association, 144
British Brick Society, 144,145
British Columbia, 108
Broaks Wood, 24,115
Bright, Dorothy Olive, 98
Bristow, Edith, George & Winifred, 58
Broyd, Harry, 124
Bruty, William George, 35,40
Bryan & Son, 115
Bulmer, 49, 126
Bulmer Brick and Tile Co. Limited, 49,143
Bulmer Brick and Tile Works, 47,50,74,81,129, 132,133,143,149
Bures, 40

C

Carder, Mary, 21
Castle, Alfred T., 105
Castle Hedingham, 13,15,17,18,20,21,24,43-45, 87,88,90,98,102,103,105,108,115,117,121
 Brick Kiln Hill, 17,23
 Crouch Green, 17,18,20,23,30,71,85,87,90-93,105,111,115,118
 Forge Green, 49
 Hedingham Castle & Estate, 17,26,32,81,87, 102,118
 Kirby Hall, 50
 Nunnery Farm, 20,118
 Nunnery Street, 17,90,94
 Pottery Cottage, 88
 Pottery Lane, 85
 Pye Corner, 21
 St. James' Street, 141
 Sudbury Hill, 49
 Trinity Cottage, 91
Castle Hedingham Parish Council, 102
Charter, Gertrude Clifford, 136
Chatten, Ernest, 141
Clare, 81
Clark, Sidney Charles, 45
Chelmsford, 131,132,144
Coggeshall, 40
Colchester Archaeological Trust, 144
Colne Engaine, 74
Colne Valley & Halstead Railway, 19,63,64,79, 87,94,96
Collier, W. H., 115
Cooke, Constance & William, 31
Cooper, Ashley, 126
Copford, 102
Corder, Alfred, 20,21,113,114,124
Corder, Alfred Cecil, 119
Corder, Alice, 105,107
Corder, Alice Agnes, 98

163

Corder, Alice Ann, 31,71,72
Corder, Alice Edith, 87,88
Corder, Alice Lucy, 133
Corder, Alice Muriel Gladys, 105,107
Corder, Annie, 112
Corder, Anthony Sudbury, 114
Corder, Beatrice, 50,58,60-62
Corder, Bert William, 43,44,65,74,98-103,139-141
Corder, Brian, 133
Corder, Caroline, 36,50,55
Corder, Cecil Edward, 133
Corder, Charles (1837-1877), 143
Corder, Charles (1859-1938), 21,85
Corder, Charlotte Eliza, 143
Corder, David, 17,111
Corder, Dorothy Olive, 98
Corder, Edith, 126,128
Corder, Edward (1818-1896), 15,128
Corder, Edward (1868-1940), 94,98,105-108, 110,112
Corder, Edward Dyson, 105,108
Corder, Edward John, 71,94,97,98,105,140,141
Corder, Edward Stanley, 98
Corder, Eliza (1830-1911), 20,115-117
Corder, Eliza (1836-1923), 21
Corder, Eliza (1842-1920), 35, 53,57
Corder, Elizabeth (1775-1853), 21
Corder, Elizabeth (1842-1873), 111
Corder, Elizabeth (1857-1935), 115
Corder, Ellen, 90
Corder, Ethel Mary, 81
Corder, Evelyn Gladys, 119
Corder, Ezekiel Thomas, 126,128,132
Corder, Frances, 143
Corder, Frank Sudbury, 114
Corder, Fred, 35,39,40,45-47,50,57-61,81,121, 139,142
Corder, George, 45,67,68,70-74,77,81,122,139
Corder, Hannah, 24,71
Corder, Harriet, 30,85,87,93,105
Corder, Harry (1873-1942), 19,29,32,33,35-50, 54,55,57-61,68,81,90,94,98,102,115,121-123, 125,139,140,142
Corder, Harry (1891-1906), 67
Corder, Henrietta Jane, 71,98
Corder, Henry, 21,35,40,45,63,115,116
Corder, Herbert Charles, 77-79
Corder, James (1798-1863), 21
Corder, James (1840-1907), 17,21,105,112
Corder, Jane, 132
Corder, Jeffrey, 21
Corder, John (1806-1880), 13,15-23,25,30, 38,83,111-113,115,117
Corder, John (1832-1907), 20,21
Corder, John (1863-1957), 35,45,58,93-98, 103,105,120
Corder, John (1876-1922), 35,40,45,53-56,81, 121,139
Corder, Joseph, 143

Corder, Kenneth Frederick, 100,103
Corder, Laura, 115
Corder, Lily, 128,132
Corder, Margaret, 114,124
Corder, Mary (1801-1871), 21
Corder, Mary (1860-1923), 82
Corder, Mary Ann (1840-1924), 105
Corder, Mary Ann (1841-1874), 126
Corder, Mary Ann (1844-1921), 114
Corder, Mary Ann (1882-1954), 128,129
Corder, Mary Hannah, 85
Corder, Myra, 126,128
Corder, Percy James, 20,40,81,98,103,104,139
Corder, Raymond John, 133,143
Corder, Robert, 17,25,30,83-85,87,90,93,102, 105,118
Corder, Sarah (1812-1883), 21
Corder, Sarah (1894-1981), 50,61
Corder, Susan (1809-1877), 30,83,115
Corder, Susan (1880-1960), 50,55
Corder, Thomas, 13,128
Corder, Walter Edward, 40,45,81,82,123,139
Corder, William (d.1792), 13,143
Corder, William (1767-1844), 21,143
Corder, William (1835-1903), 13,17,21-35,51, 53,57,58,60,63-68,71,82,83,87,100,113,115, 117,122
Corder, William (1889-1917), 129
Corder, William Dan, 74-76,139
Corder-Birch, Adrian, 144,145
Corder's Chase, 22,25,40-42
Corder's Villas, 112
Cornish, Daniel, 94
Cornish, Eli, CC.,JP., 81,95,119,139,140
Courtauld, Samuel Limited, 77
Crittalls Works, Braintree, 77
Cutts, John, 30

D

Darlington, Durham, 107
Darlington Ranch, Canada, 107,108
Downs, Arthur, 121
Downs, Charles, 121
Downs, Edith, 58
Downs, Eliza, 35,87
Downs, Emma, 121
Downs family, 13,122
Downs, Harry Arthur, 121
Downs, John, 13,18
Downs, Phoebe, 19
Downs, Sarah Ann, 17-19
Downs, Stanley, 132
Downs, William (1813-1904), 87
Downs, William (1821-1845), 18
Dowsett, Frank & Mary, 17
Drury, Alice Edith, 87,88
Drury, Fred, 87,88
Drury, Mary, 87,88

Drury, Sarah, 87
Drury, William Thomas, 87
Dyson, Agnes, 88
Dyson, Alice, 105
Dyson, Martha, 88

E

Earey, Jessie, 121
Earey, Robert, 45
Earls Colne, 74,112
East Essex Hunt, 58
Elsdon, George Thomas, 44
Eley, Thomas, 25
English, George, 126,129,132
English Heritage, 144,145
English, John Parmenter, 132
Essex County Council, 144,145
Evans, John, 30

F

Factories and Workshop Act 1871, 21
Felton, Alfred, 129
Felton, Arthur, 129
Felton, Eliza, 131
Felton family, 129,130
Felton, Harry, 130
Felton, Horace, 129
Felton, Mary, 129
Felton, Mary Ann, 129
Felton, Walter, 129,130
Finance Act 1910, 40
Finch, Albert Arthur, 45-47,125,127
Finch, Alfred Benjamin, 126
Finch, Alfred Thomas, 125
Finch, Arthur of Castle Hedingham, 105,112
Finch, Arthur (1875-1945), 136
Finch, Arthur John, 126,127
Finch, Arthur William, 125
Finch, Barnard Alfred, 127
Finch, Charles, 21
Finch, Edward Benjamin, 125,126
Finch, Elizabeth, 21
Finch, Ellen, 121
Finch, Ernest, 48
Finch family of Gestingthorpe, 13,125-128
Finch family of Hull, Yorkshire, 135-137
Finch, Gascoin Foster, 135
Finch, Gladys, 47
Finch, George (1835-1913), 15
Finch, George (1838-1892), 135
Finch, George Barnabas, 125
Finch, George Charter, 136,137
Finch, George Frederick, 126
Finch, George Henry, 125,126
Finch, George Herbert, 15
Finch, Isaac, 21
Finch, Lawrence Richard, 136

Finch, Madeline May, 137
Finch, Mary Ann, 105,112
Finch, Myra, 127
Finch, Percy Charles, 136,137
Finch, R & Sons & Co., 136,137
Finch, Richard and Sons and Co. Limited, 137
Finch, Richard, 135,136
Finch, Richard Witty, 135
Finch, Robert, 112
Finch, Sarah, 136
Finch, Thomas, 125
Finch, Thomas Ezekiel, 125,126
Finch, William, 136
Fleet, Hampshire, 107
Fletcher, James, 42,43
Friendly Societies, 139-141

G

Gatward, James, 42
Gentry, Mark, 68,71-73,94,95,98,105,119,120,
    124,139
Gepp, Ernest Edward, 121
Gepp family, 120-122
Gepp, Joseph & Sarah, 121
Gepp, Joseph Charles & Jessie, 121
Gepp, William Bernard & Gracie May, 121
Gestingthorpe, 13-15,18,19,23,36,37,45,67,83,
    111-113,125-127,129-134,140
    Audley End, 46,132
    Barracks, 133
    Church Street, 13
    Clamp, 13,134
    Crouch House Farm, 19
    Delvyns Farm, 13
    Hill Farm, 133
    Over Hall, 14,58
    Pot Kiln Chase, 13,126,130
    Wesbro and Wisborough Hill, 131
Gibson, (Arthur) Frank, 44,103
Gooch, Harry Walter William, 74
Goodchild, George, 65,100
Gosfield,
    Easter Cottage, 67
    Gosfield Hall & Estate, 32,67,70
    Park Hall Road, 32,67-71
Great Maplestead, 101
Great Northern Railway, 85
Great Yeldham, 30,56,90,99
    Great Yeldham Hall, 100
    Grove House, 63
    Lovingtons Farm, 94
    Poole Farm, 81,94
    Poole Street, 63,66
    Potters Hall, 32,63-66,100
    Whitlock Chaff Works, 66
Gurteen, Eli & Harry, 84

H

Halstead, 40,44,45,87,99
   Adam's Brewery, 116
   Bois Field, 114
   Clover's Mill, Bridge Street, 114
   Colchester Road, 114
   Courtauld's Mill, 132
   House of Correction, 70
   Old Tan Yard, 114,115
   Sudbury's Yard, 114
   Tidings Hill, 115
Halstead County Court, 121
Halstead Rural District Council, 42,99,102
Halstead Union Assessment Committee, 32
Halstead Urban District Council, 99
Hammett, Michael, 145
Hammond, Elizabeth, 111
Hampton Court Palace, 143
Hardy, Elizabeth, 21
Hardy, George & Son, 63,83
Harrington, Robert, 24
Harrod, Jack, 103
Hart, John and William, 19
Hatfield, Hertfordshire, 119
Hedingham Brick & Tile Works, 94,95,98,103,105
Hedingham Brick Company, 95
Hedingham House, Thundersley, 105-107
Hedingham Working Men's Club, 139
Hedinghams Brass Band, 98,140,141
Heels, Mary & William Jonathan, 82
Highfield Brick Works, 94,119,139
Hilsden, Agnes, 88
Hilton, Charles Augustus, 24,25
Hilton, John, 24
Howard, Arnold, 141
Howe, Ben, 103
Humber Brick Works, 137,138
Hunt, R. & Co. Limited, 112
Hunt, Reuben, 95

I

Ings Road Brick Works, 137,138
Institute of Clayworkers, 71
Ives, Caroline, 133
Ives, Frederick & Robert, 132
Ives, Jane, 132
Ives, Mary Ann, 126
Ives, Susan, 13,83

J

Jay, Mrs. James, 102

K

Kay, Mr. Justice, 30
Kendall, Annie, 88

King, Arthur George & Emma, 121
King family, 120,121
King, Frederick Charles, 121
Kingston upon Hull, Yorkshire, 135-137

L

Land Tax Assessments, 24,25
Land Value Duty Survey 1910, 40,85
Langthorne Brick Works, 68,71,73,119,124,144
Lebeau, Henry Edwin & Lilian, 126
Leonard, Thomas Herbert, 137
Lighting Order 1916, 40
Lindsay, Jack, 51,87,90
Ling, Charles Robert, 74
Little Maplestead, 44,45
Little Yeldham, 13,30,99
Long, Sir Ronald, 47
Lowe, Arthur Courtauld Willoughby, 30,32
Lowe, Col. Arthur Swann Howard, 30,32
Lowe, George Hurst Armerin, 30,32
Loyal Courtauld Lodge of Oddfellows, 140
Loyal Webster Lodge of Oddfellows, 139-142

M

Maiden Ley Brick Works, 71,77-81,120,124
Majendie family, 87,118
Majendie, James Henry Alexander, 118
Majendie, Lewis Ashurst, 32
Majendie, Musette, CBE., 81
Manor Brick Works, Thundersley, 94,98,105-110
Manor Brickworks Limited, 105,107
Marfleet, Yorkshire, 137,138
Marshall, Alfred, 30
Martin, Albert, 102
Martin, Herbert Henry, 33
Martin, Kate Edith, 133
Martin, William, 50
Metson, Alfred, 140
Michelmersh Brick Works, Hampshire, 145
Minter, Lawrence, 49,50
Minter, Peter, 56,143,149
Moss, Sarah, 21
Moulsham Brick Works, 131
Moy, Thomas Limited, 83,92,94,118,123
Museum of Practical Geology, 65

N

Newman, Jane, 13
Norfolk, Amelia, 114
Norton, James Smith, 42,45
Nott, Billy, 132
Nugent, Earl, 70

O

Osborne, Thomas, 24

P

Palmer and Corder, 44,45,98
Palmer, Charles Horace, 98
Parish, John, 24
Park Hall Road Brick Works, 67-71,122
Parker, Sarah Ann, 18
Parkeston, 144
Parr, Eliza Mary, 87
Parr, George, 87
Parr, Harriet (1816-1890), 87
Parr, Harriet (1834-1899), 85,87,93,102,105
Parr, Joseph, 87
Parr, Percy James, 43,45,102
Parr, William, 102
Parsons, Tom, 141
Philp, Cyril, 50
Post, Henrietta Jane, 98
Potters Hall Brick, Tile & Pottery Works, 63-66, 83,115
Public Health Act 1848, 19
Pudney & Son, 74,115
Purls Hill Brick Works, 95

Q

Queen Elizabeth II, 81
Quinton, Jesse, 47

R

Rayner family of Castle Hedingham, 71,77,78, 98,120,124
Rayner Brick Works & family of Gestingthorpe, 13, 14,67,125,126,129,130,132,133,140
Rayner Friendly Society, 140
Rayner, George, 73,77
Rayner, John, 13
Rayner, Mary, 131
Rayner, Phyllis, 67
Raynham, William Wright, D.C.M., 95,139
Redgewell, Albert, 95
Redgewell, George & Sarah, 71
Redgewell, Hannah, 24,71
Ripper, Charlton, 95
Ripper, (Harry) Tucker, 95,108
Ripper, Norman, 24
Rippers Joinery Works and Rippers Limited, 61, 74,77,81,87,98,108,121,124,139
Rippingale, Arthur (1864-1940), 133
Rippingale, Arthur (1884-1966), 127,133
Rippingale, Caroline, 133
Rippingale family, 131
Rippingale, Harry, 45,131-133
Rippingale, Joseph, 131
Rippingale, Kate Edith, 133
Rippingale, Lily, 132
Rippingale, Reginald Arthur, 133
Rippingale, Ruby Florence, 127
Rippingale, Samuel, 131
Rippingale, Smith, 131
Rippingale, Walter & Eliza, 131
Rippingale, Walter William, 133
Rochford Rural District Council, 105
Rogers, Zachariah, 112
Ruffle, Eliza Mary Parr, 87
Ruffle family, 103
Ruffle, Fred, 103
Ruffle, William Cousins, 87
Rulton, Harry, 46

S

Sams, Ethel Mary, 81
Savill, John, Executors of, 25
Service, Robert, 107
Sharp, George, 45
Sible Hedingham, 17,22,25,30,31,33,40,42,44-46,58,81,101-103,119,123,130,139-141,144
   Alderford Farm, 24,25
   Alderford Hall, 121
   Alderford Street, 120,123
   Alexandra Road, 42,71,103
   Assembly Rooms, 139,140
   Bay Cottage, Swan Street, 47,50,61,140
   Braintree Corner, 41,42
   Brook Farm, 77
   Church Street, 140,141
   Clay Hall Farm, 24,31
   Cobbs Fenn, 119
   Corder's Chase, 22,25,40-42
   Cut Maple, 30,42,55
   Foxborough Hill Farm and House, 24,103
   Half Moon Public House, 48
   Hawkwood Manor, 24
   High Street Green, 17
   Hole Farm, 24
   Lamb Lane, 24,25
   Liston Hall Farm, 26
   Manor of Prayors, 30,32
   New England, 94,120
   Perryfields & Pevors Farms, 32
   Potter Street, 24
   Purls Hill, 81
   Purls Hill Plantation, 96
   Queen Street, 48,71,74
   Recreation Ground, 98
   School Hill, 103
   Southey Green, 21,24,26-30,32,42,55,111,121
   Southey Green Farm, 25,41
   Starlings Hill, 24,41
   Station Road, 92
   Swan Cottage, Swan Street, 59
   Swan Street, 43,74,102,120
   Tile Kiln Farm, 24
   Tower Windmill, 24,25
   Tythings, Rectory Meadow, 50
   Warrens Farm, 26-28,31,32

Washlands Farm House, 34
Websters Meadow, 140
Wethersfield Road, 71-73,98
Sible Hedingham Parish Council, 29,98,140
Sible Hedingham Red Brick Company, 50,81, 95-97,124
Sible Hedingham Rifle Club, 98
Slythe, Isaac, 70
Smith, Benjamin, 90-92
Smith, Daniel, 24
Smith, Golden Ernest, 31
Smith, Ellen, 17,90,91
Smith, Hannah, 131
Smith, Harry, 90
Smith, James Henry, 121
Smith, Leonard, 91
Smith, Lily Maud, 91
Smith, Maud, 140
Smith, Morton & Long, 47
Smith, Philip & Sarah, 90
Smith, Susannah Ann, 122
Southey Green Brick, Tile & Pottery Works, 21, 22,24,31-62,68,71,81-83,90,94,98,113,115, 117,122,123,125
Southwark, 111
Springett, Maurice, 42,44
Stanwell, Middlesex, 107
Steggles, Sarah, 87
Steward, Alf, 103
Steward, Harry, 102
Sudbury, Suffolk, 40,58
Sudbury, Amelia, 114
Sudbury, Anthony, 114
Sudbury, George & Sons, 114
Sudbury, Louis, 114
Sudbury, Mary Ann Norfolk, 114
Sudbury, Robert & Son, 114
Sulman, F., 105
Surridge, Frank, 125
Sutton, Yorkshire, 137,138

T

Tariff Reform League, 120
Thundersley, 105-107,109,110
Toppesfield, 99
Turner, Bessie, Ellen & John, 74
Turner, Ernie, 125
Twamley, Dr. Henry Joseph, 139
Twitchett, Frank Redgewell, 81

U

Usher, Cecil & Kate, 100

V

Venables, Cuthbert Edward, 107

W

Walker, Edward, 14
Walker, Thomas, 24
Wallace, Oliver, 77
Warburton, Rev. Henry, 33
Ward, Tom, 103
Warren, Frances, 13,143
Watson, Frank, 100
Webb, Robert Lewis, 74,139
Webster, Eleanor & Elizabeth Amelia, 33,139
Webster Lodge, 139,140,142
Wendons Ambo, 144
Westrop, Alfred, 21,117
Westrop, Eliza, 117
Westrop, Samuel, 20,117
Wheeler, Henry, senior & junior, 105
Whitlock family, 63
Whitlock, Francis, 94
Whitlock, Henry Edward, 63
Whitlock, Walter, 81,94
Wickham St. Paul, 45,133
Wilding, Stanley, 102
Willett, Alice Ann, 71,72,122
Willett, Charles, 123
Willett, Daniel, 122,123
Willett family, 122,123
Willett, Harry, 45,68,122
Willett, Susannah Ann, 122,123
Willett, William (1833-1913), 31
Willett, William (1878-1981), 123,139
Willis, Ernest Savill, 140
Wiseman, Lewis, 141
Wiseman, Margaret & William James, 114,124
Workmen's Compensation Act, 121
Wood Street Potteries, 115
Worsfold, Alfred William, 30
Wright, Annie, 88

Y

Yorkshire (East Riding) County Council, 137